How to Get From 80 to 90 Without Even Trying

by Florence Ekstrand

Florence Ekstrand

Welcome Press
Mount Vernon, Washington

Published by Welcome Press, Mount Vernon, Washington
Printed and Distributed by BookMasters, Inc., Mansfield, Ohio

At your local bookstore or order from:

 BookMasters, Inc.
 P.O. Box 2139
 Mansfield, Ohio 44905
  Phone: 800-537-6727
   Fax: 419-589-4040
  e-mail: info@bookmasters.com
 Internet: http://www.bookmasters.com

ISBN 0-916871-16-9

Cover art: Kilawea Point Lighthouse, watercolor by Jean Robertson Watrous
Book design: Dona McAdam, Mac on the Hill, Seattle WA

Published in the United States of America.

To the memory of
Kathleen (Kay Rose) Ryan

"And all the stars hang high above your dwelling,
Silent, as though they watched the sleeping earth."

– Samuel T. Coleridge

PREFACE

"Maybe," said my friend Louise, "you should wait until you're ninety to write this book. You may have learned more."

I replied, "It wouldn't be the first time someone had written a book without a full grasp of the subject."

It's the truth. I have no all-encompassing insights on how I moved through the first part of my eighties nor how I will travel the rest. I am more what John Updike called a "skittish pilgrim."

But I have friends and I have learned from them and from their stories. I have stories of my own that I can draw up from reservoirs of memory and the glow lights up a day when the cedar outside my window is gray with fog and gloom.

I am learning every day from my community of faith. I am learning from people like my "earth buddy," Kay Rose, to whose memory this book is dedicated. How long did I know her, three months at most? A dozen brief conversations? My daughter wrote from Alaska, "Mother, I think your friend may have been an angel. They come for their allotted time and then go on to greater adventures. But they always leave good lessons behind." Somewhere in here I will tell you about Kay Rose.

There's scarcely one of us in our 80s who won't admit that this stretch is more of an obstacle course than a fun run. But we are signed in, we have the free T-shirt, so to speak, and the direction of the course.

This book is not a set of directives — nor even suggestions — on how to reach a particular goal. Rather, it's an encouragement to you to look to your friends and their stories, to resurrect your own good memories and actively cherish them, to absorb all that is delightful in the life around you at this moment, to laugh and wave your banner as you make this run.

If in a small way this book makes the route more pleasurable, then I'll be glad I didn't wait until I was 90.

(Some names have been changed for privacy reasons, but not the stories.)

1

I suppose we could have gotten married.

But parking at City Hall these days is very tight. Even the handicapped spaces are filled most of the time.

And I would have had to shop for a dress. It would have been like shopping for a mother-of-the-bride dress or a grandmother-of-the-groom dress.

I said, "We are two 80-somethings taking care of each other. We don't have time for all that. Besides, I have a book to write. Why don't you come and share my home?"

He said, "I love you with all my heart."

CHAPTER ONE

The Best Decade

THE SUMMER MY BROTHER ERNIE TURNED NINETY HE got a ticket for driving under the influence.

He had driven the seventy-some miles into north Minneapolis to spend the evening with his old fishing buddy, Art, and Art's wife, Neva. Ernie's use of alcohol wouldn't have classified him even as a social drinker, but that night he had "one for the road" around ten. The detour around Highway 12 was rutted and unfamiliar in the blur of headlights, and the patrolman passed just as Ernie knocked over a pair of traffic cones.

He had to come back the next week to appear in court. The patrolman began his description of the incident. "This ninety-year old gentleman —"

The judge stopped him. "Say that again?"

"This ninety-year old gentleman —"

The judge leaned forward. "Is that ninety as in nine-oh?" she demanded, incredulous.

My brother got off with a warning. "Next time, ask for coffee." As Ernie left, the judge was still murmuring, "Ninety?!"

I can remember — and not so long ago — when the word "eighty" evoked the same incredulous response in me. Eighty and still driving? Eighty and living alone? Eighty and going up two flights of stairs? Eighty and holding up his end in a conversation? Eighty and — ah — almost normal?

When I was 75, I wrote,

> "In this new world of bytes and chips,
> Of cyberspace and disks and blips,
> We seniors read each others' lips,
> An internet of faulty hips,
> And shop, thanks to our mended hearts,
> For bran flakes at our Supermarts."

Now, almost ten years later, I think, only a callow 70-something could have written something so shallow! For we have come into our eighties more fit and alert than any generation before us and more cognizant of how to stay that way! We have come into the BEST DECADE OF OUR LIVES!

Think what we have survived.

We survived being fifty when, with one turn of the calendar page, we suddenly thought we were OLD. We agonized over every gray hair, over every extra pound. We catalogued every ache and pain and put it in the file marked, "Aging." Some became grandparents — grandparents! How could we when only yesterday we had been so young? Someone coined the term, "senior moment," and we seized it as our own. We gave aberrant behavior a name: midlife crisis. The only thing worse than being fifty was knowing that sixty was just down the road.

But we survived being sixty. Today the 60-year olds are doing all the same things we did, buying backpacks and Birkenstocks and vitamins with "silver" on the bottle. They emulate the hairdos and dress of the models on the cover of *Modern Maturity*. They watch seniors on television commercials as they skip from stone to stone in a rushing stream and think, "We must do that." They sign up for all the classes their schedule will hold to be ready for the big "R" — retirement. But there's always a backward glance. Is age creeping up on us? Are we really going to be seventy?

Being 70-something wasn't easy but we survived that, too. It is perhaps the most difficult decade. Our children become middle-aged. Our grandchildren, who used to come to us with their games and stories, with their teddy bears for sleeping over, are young adults now and have lives of their own. Death begins to claim our contemporaries, even our siblings. In our sixties, we couldn't get enough of travel; in our seventies, we remembered crowded planes and long hours of delay on the tarmac and opted for travel films on TV. Many of the health problems we imagined when we were fifty became real in our seventies. After 15 minutes in almost any group the conversation turned to health care, retirement homes or nursing home insurance.

But we have survived all that! For the most part we have, as the saying goes, "our affairs in order." Our wills are up to date. The legal directives are made. Our relationship with health care providers may be more transitory than we would like but we have learned a lot about recognizing our own danger signals. We are not caring for aged parents; still, our skills as caretakers have been burnished by experience and stand ready always. Our children fuss over us but for the most part give us our space. Our grandchildren have become wonderful adults and send thank-you notes.

We are less concerned with time. Time is ever-flowing and passing from eighty to eighty-one is simply a mark on the calendar.

It has nothing to do with our energy level, our expectations, our plans or dreams. "Time is important only on a daily level," says my Swedish friend Per. "Morning, because the morning paper arrives, evening because the evening paper comes."

We are more comfortable with ourselves. We are less critical and more accepting than we were at fifty, less opinionated than we were at sixty. But we feel free to express ourselves, sometimes perhaps a little too free. But what we say is less confrontive, gentler perhaps, than in other decades. We have taken the good Francis's prayer to heart: we change the things we can, we no longer wring our hands over what can't be changed and God has given most of us the wisdom to tell the difference.

Not that we are Pollyannas, seeing all things as good. But we can relate to the boy in the story that President Reagan liked to tell when the going got rough:

"When the boy came down on Christmas morning and found nothing under the tree but a pile of manure, he began to dig through it. 'Somewhere in here,' said the boy, 'there has got to be a pony!'"

We have become realists. We know that life is not always fair, that rain falls on the just and unjust alike. It is easier to accept this than it is to accept our limitations. We still dream, but we make fewer long range plans, though my brother Ernie bought a brand-new Buick when he turned 84.

"We are a rare and privileged breed," says my friend Marv, recalling his growing up years in the 30s and 40s. "We may not like everything that's swirling around us but we refuse to return to the past, to become cynical or immobilized or isolated." We are not knee-jerk patriots; love of country has been part of our blood and bones since childhood.

And better than any other age group, we are equipped to

handle disaster, even privation, should it come our way. For ours is the generation that fought World War II on many fronts. Tom Brokaw paid a long-overdue tribute to those men and women in his book, *The Greatest Generation,* and now young people are beginning to ask us, "How could you handle all that worry and loss?"

What younger people fail to realize is that we came into that conflagration already honed and toughened by a disaster almost as painful as the war — the Great Depression and the years of terrible drought.

A man whose destroyer was bombed out from under him at Pearl Harbor told me, "I was from Oklahoma and the day I turned 17 and joined the Navy and got on a ship was the first time I got up from the dinner table feeling full."

We are the generation whose parents lost jobs and homes and farms, who knew banks that closed, who saw childhood friends sent to live with relatives on farms, where there would at least be milk and eggs. We spent our high school years in hand me downs and made-over outfits. A big date was a ten-cent movie and a small bag of popcorn. Our big purchase of the week might be a 25-cent gadget that mended our one pair of silk stockings so the runs barely showed.

It left a mark. Are we too cautious? Uneasy with anything, however small, that suggests affluence?

Perhaps. But those years also left a strength so deeply imbedded, so much a part of us, that there's not much can frighten us. Use the expression, "Come what may," and almost any 80-something is apt to add, at least to himself, "I can handle that, too."

And one thing we know. We have a sweep of history that no generation before us lived long enough to experience, for most of us connect with six generations! I remember three of my grandparents; in Sweden they lived in an agrarian society barely touched by the Industrial Revolution. My father began farming with horses, ended with a tractor and never set foot on an airplane. Our grand-children and great-grandchildren? At 80-something we can't even imagine their world at our age.

It's true, we look backward more than we look forward. And why not? We've spent 80 years of our life there! But it's also true that the present becomes more precious and endearing to us for each year that passes. The joy of being part of this present time transcends every worry about the future. It lends a radiance to ev-ery encounter, whether it's discovering the first lilac bud of the season or unexpectedly running into an old friend in the produce section of the local supermarket.

Given the past and all we programmed into it, given the present with its challenges and the future with its possibilities, this could truly turn out to be the Best Decade of all!

2

It wasn't that simple, of course.

I saw him first at the after-church coffee on a bright May morning. He was leaning against a wall, cup in hand. He was tall but slumped, pale, looking somehow shrunken, like a leaf beginning to curl.

I greeted him briefly, then found three or four other widows. "Please go visit with that elderly man over there. I think he's very lonely."

The next Sunday he was there again, alone. We chatted briefly. When I turned to go he said, "Thank you for talking with me." It gave my heart a wrench and I turned back. I asked a few questions. It turned out his wife had died a year ago. He himself had been ill and depressed. Both his sons lived at a distance. The previous Sunday morning, he said, it was as if his wife spoke to him and said, "There's a church at the top of the hill, get yourself up there." I told him how happy we were to have him and got a brief, flashing smile.

He came to a concert. I said, "Would you like to sit with us?" He came to the church picnic and said, "May I sit with you?" We learned he was Boston Irish and a retired Navy officer. I looked around for just the right woman for him. I had no time for a man in my life — I had a book to write.

That summer I went to Denmark and Sweden for five weeks. Returning, I came out of customs and he was waiting, a big grin on his Irish face.

"How in the world did you know I was on this flight?"

He looked like the cat that swallowed the canary. "I have my sources." He was different, erect now, smiling, with color in his face. "I'm taking you to lunch before I bring you home," and he picked up my bag.

It was the first of many lunches, many stories. He told me about his father, who had driven an ice cream delivery wagon in Lynn, Massachusetts. He told me about the nuns in his school — Jumping Julia, Sister Ricarta who became "Ricci." Throwing snowballs at the steam trains' locomotives. The ship with enlistees pulling out of Portsmouth, heading for the Pacific in summer, 1938, Pearl Harbor three years later. The bombers passed over the USS Case but he watched the carnage.

We sent birthday and Christmas cards, "To a Good Friend." Signed them "Sincerely," or "All my best." But when I bought him a bright green St.Patrick's Day card, I thought, this is ridiculous.

We were in my living room and he showed me the green shirt he had bought for the day.

"Look," I said, holding the card, "these man-woman relationships are so awkward. I sign almost all my cards, 'With love,' but with you it feels uncomfortable. And that's silly, because I really do love you."

I thought he'd say yes, it would be very nice to sign our cards "with love." Instead he almost leaped from his chair and lifted me from the sofa into a huge bear hug.

"If you only knew how I've been trying to find a way to tell you how much I love you!" He titled my head back and kissed me. He drew me down on the sofa. "I'm going to sit here and kiss you again and again and tell you how much I love you."

And he did. And I forgot I had a book to write.

CHAPTER TWO

"Dr. Livingston, I Assume?"

NO, LORD STANLEY DID NOT SAY THAT. HE SAID, "I presume?" Here are two words whose meanings are so close that the dictionary uses one as a definition of the other. And yet when we use them we instinctively feel the difference.

To assume something is to take for granted that a statement or situation is as it seems, that it is true. It seems to me Stanley could well have assumed that the man before him was the intrepid Dr. Livingston. After all, he was known to be in this part of Africa, there was word of him at every jungle outpost, he had a description of the man if not a photo — and how many Englishmen with a company of bearers were, after all, making their way through the bush?

But even in the jungle Stanley bore the innate reserve of the Englishman. To assume that this khaki-clad figure before him was the legendary adventurer that he had been seeking for weeks was too direct, too brash. He would instead presume, which has the feeling of anticipating, as if waiting for an assurance.

This comes sharply to mind as I make the most important statement of this book: I cannot assume that you have a spiritual roadmap for moving through your eighties. But I can presume that you do. For it would have been very, very difficult to have come this far without one.

It may be a strong personal faith, whatever the persuasion. It may be a faith rooted in childhood, or a new revelation born of study and seeking. You may be a part of a spiritual community that meets all your needs, or you may read and meditate on your own. You may have found your bond with God through some personal revelation, or you may gain a one-ness with others through a liturgical worship, or you may see in great music and art the spirit of the Divine.

I cannot assume this of you, but I can presume it.

On the other hand, not everyone entering their eighties may have a spiritual roadmap. You may have had one but it has been creased too many times, the edges are ragged. Colors have faded.

If this is the case, let me share one with you. It is very simple. Only the main outline of the map is there; all the comforting country roads, the scenic drives, the historic crossroads, the exits to breath-taking viewpoints, these will all come to you as you travel.

Actually, the roadmap is in the form of a prayer, a table grace:

> "Come, Lord Jesus, and be our guest,
> And let these gifts to us be blest."

"Come."

It is a straightforward invitation that may seem hardly necessary. For the Presence is always there, the all-encompassing love of the eternal God surrounds us whether we acknowledge it or not. But we have a need to reach out and touch and relate and know.

We need to see and feel an expression of that great love. And so we say, "Come, meet me where I am."

To meet that ultimate expression of love is, for many of us, to meet the Nazarene prophet.

Even in our egalitarian society, the words, "Lord Jesus," touch us. There is the sense of dominion in the highest, finest sense of the word. And in that dominion we find our own place: student with teacher, apprentice with master, follower with leader, the rescued with the savior, the needy with one who empowers.

"Be our guest." This carries us beyond the door. Come in and be part of my life. Sit down, talk with me. This guest comes immediately and without long acquaintance. He may make demands you never dreamed of. He may say, "Surprise me!" As your guest he will walk with you through all the hard places. He knows. He has been there. And unlike other guests, he will not leave you.

"Let these gifts to us be blest." A Norwegian couple and I spent a whole morning trying to translate a Norwegian table prayer into English. All went well until the last line. The nearest I could come was that we asked God to help us share our bounty with the less fortunate. But Alf and Gudrun pushed for something nearer to what the Norwegian implied: that God lays upon us an obligation to share our bounty with the less fortunate. It was more than we could fit into the meter but the message lingers.

This last line here is also a translation, a natural progression of the first. As God enters our lives as a guest, we come to acknowledge that the meal and all that it implies are gifts to us. It is faith translated into both gratitude and action. As the gifts are blessed by God (as our spirit widens, as our faith grows, as our spirituality is enriched) there is no escape: God has moved in and we find ourselves sharing that love, forgiveness, acceptance and help with everyone around us.

For all that this decade is our best, our vision and hearing are often diminished. If there was ever a time to polish the clarity of our spiritual vision, it is now. Find a spiritual fellowship, nurture the one you may already have, read things that inspire, search out people that can help and encourage you, pray, meditate, listen. And remember that every road map, as it leads us to our destination, also opens to us the splendor, warmth and joy of the lands and people we pass on the way.

3.

Three weeks later it was all over.

The book I had bought him, the books I had loaned him, the green Hallmark with the Legend of St. Patrick, they were all in a paper shopping bag left at my back door while I was in church that Sunday morning.

I called my friend Louise. "I need to talk to someone. Can you come over? Bring cookies."

He was frightened, of course. The sailor who had fueled his pitching destroyer in the middle of a typhoon, the officer who had positioned and fired three nuclear bombs into outer space as part of Project Argus, the steely-eyed executive, was frightened.

"It wouldn't be fair to you," he'd begun saying. Age, triple bypasses, prostate surgery had all taken their toll. That arousal of passion that first surprising day held no promise of a physical relationship to follow.

"Look," I told him, "I am a year older than you. I love you because you are a dear and wonderful person. You are my best friend."

"And suppose we were to get married." He was off on another tack now. "And suppose I became very ill — and given my health history I probably will — and suppose I had to be cared for in a nursing home for a very long time. They'd take everything I had and then everything you had. I know people it's happened to — " and he began to catalog them.

This man isn't listening to me, I thought with annoyance. I wonder if he ever listens to me. And are these just excuses? Does he think I'm like the woman in the senior center who had offered him protection

*from all the other women who were eyeing his pristine 1983
Oldsmobile and his Harris tweed coat? The nerve of him! I need to
at least point out that he's paying no attention to what I say.*

*It was the first display I'd seen of his Irish temper. He grabbed his
jacket, thanked me for the afternoon and strode out. He was not in
church the next morning.*

*"I don't need this man," I told Louise, "and he doesn't need me.
But he desperately needs that church up there, and if he walks out
on me I'm afraid he'll walk out on the church as well."*

*"Especially," observed Louise dryly, "after getting up at the St.
Patrick's luncheon and announcing he'd found the woman he truly
loved."*

*I don't suppose our congregation is much different from any other
community of faith. But it is a loving, caring group, and in that
loving and caring Larry had blossomed. It was as if he had found
an expression for his faith, a faith rooted in his Catholic childhood,
one that had carried him through danger and illness and uncertainties and the despair of his wife's final illness. He smiled. He
greeted everyone warmly. He sat in the back pew ("If they have to
carry me out they won't have so far to go") and people stopped to
shake his hand and perhaps share an Irish joke. He remembered the
small children's birthdays. He bought a book of riddles and every
Sunday during the coffee hour the children clustered around him to
see if he could stump them. He took the pastor to lunch at his favorite restaurant. He was unfailingly the gentleman. When our friend
Geneva began using a cane he was quick to see that she was always
settled in a comfortable chair with her cup of coffee. For all of this I
loved him.*

"But I don't need him," I repeated. "I've done very well alone for twelve years. Besides, I have a book to write." We drank our coffee and ate our cookies. But when she left and the house was very still, I felt as if someone close to me had died.

It was Thursday morning before he called. His voice was hesitant. "I thought you might hang up on me. I'm so sorry. I don't know what got into me. I get a little crazy sometimes, I get to thinking about things and — "

Finally I broke in. "Why don't you take me to lunch today?"

CHAPTER THREE

The Day Connie Shot the Squirrel

AGE EIGHTY A GOOD TIME TO MAKE CHANGES? OH, absolutely!

At this age, we are in a perfect setting to make changes — changes in our outlooks, our attitudes, our interests, in the people we spend time with, in ourselves and our possibilities.

So many other things are out of the way now and we finally have time to think about ourselves. We can take stock of ourselves. We can step back, outside of ourselves as it were, and look at this 80-something that lives inside our skin.

And when we do, it dawns on us that we have spent these 80-some years becoming what we are and we had no plan!

I hear you protest, Oh, but I did! My faith guided me, my spirituality, my mother, that special teacher, my wife, my husband, my years in the military, that unique pastor, my college years, my field of work.

These are all influences. They helped make us what we are. But they were not a plan. And when we say that "God had a plan for my life," I think what we are really saying is this: God helped me throughout my life to be open to influences for good, gave me courage to run with the ideas that came to me or that good people placed before me. But we were also buffeted by the "whims of outrageous fortune," for good or for ill. And we reacted for good or for ill, and not always according to our plan.

Our generation did not plan to be drafted into World War II. We did not plan the hurts that made us wary of being close to anyone. We did not plan the losses that left tinges of bitterness. For many, health problems have shattered long-laid plans. Some feel adrift, others feel captive to old habits.

At 80-something we are on a sort of plateau. We can look back over the influences that shaped us, over the small scars left by things beyond our control — or in spite of our control. And eighty is a good time to plan changes.

It might be as simple as being more open to others, less timid, less concerned with "What will people say?"

My friend Pat is a case in point.

Growing up at a time when teaching and nursing were the standard careers for women, Pat chose nursing. She was good at it. She organized and taught birthing classes. Thanks to her efforts, a community college in our area was the first to offer classes in midwivery and she was the first teacher. She raised five children of her own, all the time writing in professional journals.

But Pat had a mother who was almost fanatical about reading, and Pat was steeped in the classics and in poetry. When her children were grown, her life began to change. Her own spirituality grew in importance. She took dance lessons, she sang in a quintet. She helped young artists market their paintings. She found time to walk on the beach. She wrote poetry.

Then her health became troublesome and she moved to a retirement home that should have been ideal. It was close to the symphony hall, to the ballet, to the art museums, all the things she loved. But those staid and stolid Presbyterians were not ready for a free spirit like Pat. How could you take seriously a woman who wrote poetry about a single constellation peering through her bedroom window, "Orion, the voyeur?" She felt isolated. She grew timid, feeling her dress, her attempts at conversation, her very person made her an interloper.

"Then one evening a man came in to play the piano in the lobby and there was quite a gathering. He played all those old songs that Benny Goodman and Glenn Miller had played when John and I were dating. He was playing, '...when your heart's on fire, smoke gets in your eyes...' and I don't know what got into me but I went up to the piano and began to sing! I sang that song, and another, and then another. Oh, I felt so free! And people came up to me and said how glad they were I had done it. They didn't ask me to do it again but I felt I had broken through a small wall."

"Change," wrote William Wordsworth more than two centuries ago, "yields amazing recompense."

My friend Connie, who is barely 75, says she is "working at becoming eccentric." I think this may have started the day she shot the squirrel from the balcony of her second floor condo.

She had been feeding the birds from a feeder on her balcony but was at her wits' end to know how to keep the squirrels from gobbling up all the bird feed. Finally, she went out and bought a BB gun.

"Not meaning to hurt them, mind you, but I thought a BB whizzing by their ears would be something they'd remember."

The next morning she had no more filled the feeder than the biggest squirrel was sitting right in the middle of it. This was the time to teach him a lesson. She took aim and fired.

Unfortunately her aim was not good and the squirrel fell off the balcony. Connie raced down the stairs, her heart pounding. Not only was the squirrel lying lifeless on the ground but an austere elderly man stood looking down on it.

"I panicked. I couldn't admit I'd actually shot it! I said, 'I don't know, it was just sitting on the railing and then it just — it just fell over.'"

"Definitely dead," said the man.

Connie ran back upstairs and brought down a length of paper toweling. The man wrapped the squirrel in it and together they walked to their dumpster. She returned the BB gun to the hardware store. Shortly after that she moved to Seattle, where I met her.

Too bad. If Connie really wanted to establish her eccentricity for all time she could have thrown herself on the ground and wept over the squirrel. She could have produced a splendid box to lay it in. By then a small crowd would have gathered. The man could have found a spade and they might all have proceeded to a far corner of the yard to give it burial. Even in a highly mobile society, she would have been remembered in that building.

"Eccentric, you know — the woman in 204, but a wonderfully kind heart."

A Hospice worker told me, "Never box yourself in. The older we grow, the more we need new adventures, new outlooks." It may be as little as sitting at a different window, looking at a different street. Health and mobility permitting, it may be as much as an Elderhostel trip or an African safari. When my late friend May was 83, she rode a horse down into the valley of Dead Sea; when she was 85, she rode a camel — true, it was in California. It may be renting challenging videos instead of watching the same TV shows every day, every week. Or joining a study group or discussion group on a topic that is completely new to you. Or searching out new volunteer opportunities. Or reading "Charlottes's Web" or the "Oz" books or other classics you read to your children but have long since forgotten.

Some of the things we may think of changing, like being more kind or gentling our tone of voice or learning to be a better listener, may have to do with how we want to be remembered. Our perception of people, especially of family members who are gone, often has little to do with who they really were.

One of those late winter storms had moved in the day Barbara and I sat over lunch in Charlie's at Shilshole Marina. Borne on a howling wind, the rain dashed against the windows and ran in torrents. Rows of boats bobbed like corks in their blue plastic shrouds, punctuated only by masts that swayed crazily. We could not see as far as the breakwater. People coming in shook water from their Pacific Trail jackets and those leaving went with reluctance.

I had always admired Barbara's shrewdness and unfailing good judgement. A single woman who had always guarded her privacy, she was a mathematician. Until her retirement she had worked as an analyst for a large manufacturing firm. She had just come from visiting an aged aunt in a nursing home in Phoenix.

"I never really knew Aunt Abbie because she and Uncle Ted never lived in one place long enough to go visit them," She paused, watching the gulls dive past the window and then, carried on an upward gust, disappear into the rain. "But there was something that really made me want to look her up now. Uncle Ted's been gone for two years and Abbie's not too well.

"'Poor Abbie' — that's all I ever heard. I used to think it was part of her name. The family always said Poor Abbie, Uncle Ted dragged her all over the country. Poor Abbie, she lived in a truck in the desert, or in a trailer park by a dam Uncle Ted was helping build. Poor Abbie this and Poor Abbie that.

"Well." Barbara laid down her fork. "Abbie really wanted to talk. She told me what a wonderful life she's had, and her face just glowed when she talked about it. She told of all the places she and Ted had seen, the Grand Canyon and the salt flats in Baja California and the Indians' fishing platforms on the Columbia River before the dams were built. She told how once, on the road, they'd bought a lamb from a rancher and he'd dressed it out and they roasted it on a willow spit by the Missouri River. They met Georgia O'Keefe before she was famous. Abbie laughed when she told of sewing red checked curtains for one trailer after another as they traded up. They had so much fun."

Barbara grew quiet, watching the wild rain. At last she picked up her fork. "Maybe," she said, "my life would have been better if I hadn't been so damned analytical."

I asked a few friends how their personalities had changed after reaching eighty.

"I'm not afraid to say no any more," said one. Another laughed and said, "I'm not afraid to say yes. I tell people, I may not do this perfectly but I'll try."

Walter added, "I'm more willing to use my imagination and try to understand new ideas. I read somewhere that reasoning is a mix of history, knowledge and imagination. Well, in eighty years we accumulated a lot of the first two, now maybe we can use our imaginations."

Oscar Wilde, a master at creating an artificial persona, insisted that we have layered ourselves with one sham personality after another and that if we peeled them all away we would find — nothing.

How much more heartening these words from retired Archbishop Raymond Hunthausen of the Seattle Archdiocese. At an Advent retreat in 1994 he reminded the group,

"There is a child in us that must stay alive if we are to grow in holiness. It is the same child that Jesus placed in our midst when He told us that we could hardly expect to handle heaven unless we became like that child. The tired adult in us often needs to be reminded that we are in charge of that child. You and I have the power to let it live or to bring about its early death."

Then he read one of his own poems, *On the Morality of Hanging on to Teddy Bears,* which ends with this,

> "The child in me
> longs to touch
> all of the adults I know
> with the magic of little-ness
> and perform that green miracle
> of enabling them to see
> that it is not too late
> to live happily ever after,
> the problem is so simple
> they could miss it.
> Their teddy bears
> They have thrown too far
> And desperately they need them."

4.

But things had changed, if ever so subtly. We apologized to each other. We kissed and made up. But we were both a bit wary. He handled it by being bluff and hearty, I handled it by throwing myself into my own pursuits. I weeded my flowerbeds and set annuals in the spaces where tulips and daffodils and anemones had bloomed. We talked now and then about making some kind of plans for our future but our conversations were more guarded now, procrastinating, as if we had all the time in the world to plan.

But sometimes life itself makes decisions for us. Larry's leg pain became so nagging that the doctors finally decided the only thing to do was to replace the knee with an artificial one. His sons were encouraging and supportive, but living as they did at a distance, there was no way he could go to either one to recuperate.

"You can't be alone in your apartment after surgery," I told him. "Come here for the first few days."

But the incision broke open in the hospital and an infection set in. The long "wound," as they called it, had to heal from the outside edge inward, a process that meant more days in the hospital and a long stay in a rehabilitation center. By the time he came home I had learned to dress the wound. Over the weeks we measured the healing in millimeters and celebrated each gain with strawberry sundaes.

We said our prayers together morning and evening. It was the prayer Larry and his wife had prayed and when he sometimes forgot and slipped her name in in place of mine I felt a great caring for her. "God bless my Florence, God bless me. Give us peace, health, happiness and love and friendship for each other." After a while he dropped the "friendship."

I don't remember exactly how or when it came about, but there was a time when we looked at each other and said, "This is it. This is where we belong. Here. Together." It was as simple as that.

CHAPTER FOUR

Change of Address

IN THE FARM COMMUNITY OF MY CHILDHOOD, THERE was still one old couple who drove a horse and buggy. They rented out their forty acres of fields, kept chickens and planted a big potato patch. They would live there till they died, first one, then the other.

Down the road and around the corner lived Augusta, who was also old and had been old as long as anyone had known her. Her three-room house stood on the edge of a small lake choked with reeds and lily pads. She lived "on the county" and the kindness of her neighbors. She was afraid of only two things in this life, chimney fire and pneumonia. She died of the latter.

Most of the really old people I knew then — and people over sixty were old — lived with someone, mostly with a married child. I remember my own grandmother and I associate her with our kitchen. She and I sat at the oilcloth-covered table and ate oatmeal after the others had gone their busy ways. If we spoke it was in Swedish. Both my grandfathers lived with us. One re-soled shoes, the other sharpened knives and scythes on the round grinding stone that stood in the yard. There were few options for those past their working years.

Today the options for the elderly are almost bewildering.

Boots chooses to live on a small island at the end of a long inlet into Prince of Wales Island in Southeast Alaska. She is the only resident on the island. Her nearest neighbors are a small native Alaskan community on the Prince of Wales coast, two or three miles away by water.

Boots heats her two-room house with wood gathered from the sea, plus a winter supply cut and split by a woodcutter from the mainland. Her water supply comes from rain and from a small spring at some distance. When her only island neighbor moved away, Boots bought a two-way radio and with it she orders her groceries. When the mail plane comes once a week, the groceries are lifted onto her shoreline along with the mail pouch. Understandably, her children would like to see her move to town.

"But where would I see the things I see here?" she asks. She tells of watching an eagle swoop down into the water to dig his talons into a big king salmon. So big, in fact, that no matter how hard the eagle flailed his wings he simply could not get airborne. Nor could he drop the salmon; when an eagle's talons grab a prey they cannot loosen their grip until they get their prey on solid ground.

"So the eagle kind of swam his way to my shore and dropped the salmon and then got startled and soared away. I walked out and picked up the fish and waved my thanks to the eagle."

Few of us have — or would choose — so adventurous a retirement into our eighties. More of us are like my friend Mabel who, after being injured in a fall down a flight of stairs, moved into a retirement home whose facilities included assisted living and skilled nursing care. But when her health improved dramatically, Mabel made the often heard comment: "It's nice but I think I moved too soon."

Another couple realized they, too, had moved too soon. The regimen of mealtimes, the checking in and out at the desk, the long, almost sepulchral halls, were not for them. Fortunately, they realized it while they could still be refunded their down payment and they made a second move — to an apartment.

When his wife died, my old neighbor Al, afflicted with a deteriorating muscular disease, chose to move to a retirement home in the small town near the island home where they had spent the past ten years. Here would be people who shared common interests, who loved the water and the island as he did.

"They all talk at mealtime," he says now, "but then they go to their rooms and shut the doors. There's absolutely no social life. It's very lonesome." He's handling it by joining two senior centers, one in the town and one on the island, and keeping up activities in his church.

Eleanor is a spunky, independent 90-year-old who always declared, "They'll have to carry me feet first out of this house!" They did, literally, when a back problem became debilitating. In the hospital she fought to go home. But on the day she finally realized she could no longer live at home, even with help, she put the same dogged determination into making the most of the home her nieces found for her. A week after she moved in I phoned. "Oh, this is a lovely place and they are so good to me. I don't care what they do about the house, I don't want to worry about it."

I always wanted to grow old like Gert, who lived a block down the hill from me in a neat white bungalow with a backyard full of flowers and a small white dog. In autumn she raked bags of leaves that drifted down from the Lombardy poplars in the alley. Often she walked the two steep uphill blocks to the bus stop. In her late eighties, she looked like a fashion plate. Everything matched, earrings, brooch, blouse, suit, bracelet, shoes, purse.

Her daughter planned a 90th birthday party for her at the Queen Anne Café. But when we arrived there was no Gert. The previous afternoon she had stepped off a curb, turned her foot, fallen and had broken a hip. She has been in a nursing home ever since.

We stood around drinking punch and eating cake and talking about Gert, saying things like, "You never know" and "It happens so fast." My own plans for living out the eighties like Gert suddenly had an "if" before them.

Many of us even in our eighties are simply procrastinating about paring down our lives. And it's not bad, for procrastination can be productive. Even as we live in our familiar pattern, we can do the prep work for something else. We can explore our options, talk to friends and acquaintances, get opinions. Do I want to make two moves, first an apartment, then assisted living? What about costs? Are my finances in order? Do I want to be near my familiar area or do I want to make it easier for my family to visit me?

Are records, phone and address lists easily located if they have to be moved by someone other than myself? How much can I pare down on possessions? (Don't get rid of too much — you need treasured things around you to sustain and nourish you.) But the basement accumulation? The things you haven't had out of boxes for forty years? The 1983 bank statements? We don't want anyone to find — as has happened — a four-foot stack of frozen meal trays!

If you have already made a move to a different form of residence, a different lifestyle, you have made what is likely the most difficult move you have ever made. But it can also be challenging, rewarding and — with a little work — exhilarating!

The best advice for settling in may be this comment from a friend of a friend: "All these new people closing in around me! I'm going to look at them as I did my hearing aids when I first got them: they are my friends and not my enemies!"

But change is always hard. And it's especially hard when it's a sudden change, usually precipitated by a health problem. In a moment, it seems, all the familiar surroundings are gone, the familiar people, even the smells and touch of familiar things. Our natural reaction is to begin to mourn our loss — "I loved my house so! Why did I have to part with those tools that were my father's, the big bedroom set we started out with? I can't bear to look out and not see the park or my neighbor's apple tree."

I think it is best to meet this as we meet a death; head right into it, painful as it may be.

This is how it is now. I am in new surroundings and it can be wonderful! Here are suggestions I have gleaned from my friends who have made a move.

With all the changes, we may have to make one more: attitude. Use your reserve of patience and acceptance. Take time to find the good in your dinner partner. Overlook what seem like slights; it may be nothing more than faulty eyesight, shyness or a slow reaction to someone new. Take time to listen; there will be time later to talk. Smile more. Respond warmly to overtures but don't let yourself be boxed in. Explore your new surroundings but also explore your new neighbor's interests and concerns.

Find your niche. In doing so you may find yourself. Maybe you're more outgoing than you ever thought you were. Maybe you're such a good listener that people will come to you for reassurance. If you have a skill or talent, offer it to help someone else.

Become a storyteller. Oh, not one who tells the same stories over and over, but the one that draws others out to share their stories. It is too easy for conversations to settle on weather and ailments and go no further.

When my old friend, Anna Hought, turned 95 and went to live with a granddaughter, she and the 85-year old woman across the street became fast friends. Every afternoon, after naps, they would join one another for coffee or tea.

"We got tired of talking about the weather," Anna told me. "So each day we took turns picking a topic to talk about. We talked about pastors we had known and doctors we had know. We talked about trips. And baking. But we always took turns starting it."

Without the yard work, without the household chore, often without meals to prepare, you have that great gift: TIME.

This is the time to indulge yourself in doing all the things you never found time for before. Many senior residences offer computer classes and the eighties are not too late to begin e-mailing your grandchildren. Make additions to the family history. If arthritis makes writing or even typing difficult, get a simple tape recorder and ignore the awkwardness of talking out loud without a live audience. My friend Len learned to knit at 82 and turned out bright stocking caps for the Salvation Army Christmas baskets.

Take advantage of what your particular residence has to offer: day trips, study groups, conversation groups, art lessons. Poetry groups can be especially stimulating for, as poet Stephen Crane once put it, "the poet articulates nature," and a great deal more.

Pat's poetry group at the retirement home was a haven for her. I joined her one day. The leader, a stocky, graying man who had been a high school teacher, passed out copies of Walt Whitman's poems. His wife, I learned, had died the night before, a release from a long illness. He had insisted on carrying on the class; I think it was a healing act.

He read the poems himself, which was good for he read with

feeling. We came at last to "A Noiseless Patient Spider." It seemed a comfortable poem to discuss. One of the women had lived on a ranch and she talked of the varieties of spiders she would discover in their barns. Several who had had gardens remembered going out in the morning to find dew sparkling on a perfect web. Several spoke of patience. How patient the spider was, to spin that long thread only to have it destroyed, and then to spin again. Yes, patience was what the poem was about.

But the leader pressed for more. What about the spider "exploring the vacant, vast surrounding?" Did the spider know where the other end of her filament would touch? Did the spider have a plan? Or did she trust the breeze to carry the filament where it would?

And what of the second part? What was Whitman saying when he spoke of "the bridge you will need?" A bridge? A web?

But the group grew silent. Perhaps it was too real today, the bridge to — where? Perhaps if it had been more familiar territory, like Genesis or Matthew.

Or perhaps they were only tired, for the hour was up. We kept our copies. On my way home on the No.3 bus I read the poem over and over. And I wondered.

Do we build our webs again and again over the years, one gossamer filament at a time, widening and expanding each time? As changes come, as one dewy web after another is swept down and we begin another, do we ever know where that bridge will lead, where the "gossamer web" will take us?

What does it matter, I thought as I paid my fare at my own stop and walked down the hill. What does it matter if the spider has a plan? What does it matter as long as I feel the "anchor holding" with each filament of change I cast on the breeze?

5.

That late summer was one of those rare seasons that seldom come to the Pacific Northwest. The sun shone day after day and the earth responded, holding a soft and pervasive warmth far into the evening. Night after night, dinner over, we sat on the open back porch and watched the stars come out. I watered the flowerbeds almost daily now and the smell of wet geraniums and the nasturtiums that had seeded themselves floated up from the lower deck.

"You've never seen the stars until you've seen them at sea." Larry's left leg, still encased in a brace so the wound would not break open again, was propped on another chair. It seemed as if he had always been here, had come with the house, perhaps. "All through the war we ran without lights, of course. You'd be on watch in that blackness and the stars — there are millions of them! I wish you could see them from the sea."

"I remember them from growing up in the country. On the coldest nights in winter they seemed to shimmer. I remember the harvest moon and sometimes the Northern Lights. Did you ever see them from the East Coast?"

We watched lights of planes heading for Vancouver or Anchorage or Tokyo; some we thought were taking the polar route to Copenhagen. We told each other stories, many stories, for we had no shared story that went back much more than a year.

We told of our childhoods, he with the Ganey twins next door in a predominately Irish — American city hugging the Atlantic coast, a city where St. Joseph's Church held eight Masses every Sunday and the town band played every Sunday afternoon in a park next to Goldfish Pond. I told him of the solitude of a Minnesota farm, my siblings much older than I, of fishing in lakes and hunting jackrabbits with my brothers in winter, and going to town on Saturday nights in summer to hear the town band play in a little park near the railroad depot.

He was one of three officers who did the preliminary work on the Navy's nuclear submarine base at Bangor, across the bay from Seattle. There had been an ammunition depot there during World War II. "But when we came it had gone back to mostly woods and brush, lots of deer, a bear or two. Some day we'll catch the ferry — I'd like to show you Bangor."

But I had been to Bangor. In the early 1980s my friend Diane and I had gone there to join a Ground Zero peaceful protest against bringing nuclear warheads in by rail from Texas. I chose not to tell him.

It was a golden late summer. There was a serenity about those evenings that worked a magic for us, a bonding. We didn't speak of it, he was not given to abstract terms and I tend, too often perhaps, to hold things inside. It was enough to say, "I love you" from some deeper level than we had found before.

Then both darkness and the evening chill came earlier. We moved inside, leaving behind the winking planes, the sweep of stars and the low hum of traffic over the Aurora Bridge.

CHAPTER FIVE

Gabriella, Who Danced on the Ceiling

SHE ARRIVED UNANNOUNCED, UNINVITED AND certainly unwelcome. She was simply there one morning when I wakened. She was sailing across the ceiling like a shooting star, making great swoops and dips and swings. When I sat up she moved to the wall in front of me. I turned my head and she went with me. Make no mistake, she wanted to hog the spotlight.

She was small, lithe and dark in color. There was something of a ballerina in the way she moved, especially on the uncluttered stage of the bedroom ceiling. When I realized I was not going to be rid of her I gave her a name. "Gabriella" seemed appropriate, a graceful, swooping name.

Gabriella stayed for three or four days and then was gone. Various of her relatives have come and gone since then and now I pay little attention. Let them have their time in the spotlight.

Gabriella was, of course, a "floater." My ophthalmologist describes them as "tiny clumps of jell that break loose from the vitreous, the clear, jelly-like substance that forms the eyeball." In that semi-liquid they float, and when they settle in front of the pupil they cast sharp shadows on anything the eye sees. As the eye moves, they move.

Gabriella is one small example of the vicissitudes that have made us 80-somethings experts in a vital art — coping.

We began to hone our skills in coping when we were in our seventies. The health problems we had worried about in our fifties were beginning to be real. And we had the mistaken idea that if we complained about them it would elicit sympathy and sympathy is what we were after.

We were dead wrong! If complaining produced a brief murmur of sympathy, it also opened the floor to everyone within earshot to do the same. Invariably, their problems were always worse, of longer standing and much more exotic.

Take back problems. If you dare to mention you have two herniated disks that are giving you real anguish, half a dozen people will tell you that their backs "went out" twice in the last three weeks. Backs are always "going out." Where do they go? Do they go in search of the socks that have "gone out" through the secret exit in the dryer?

Complaining becomes a game of one-upmanship. True, we need to be open with family and friends about things that hurt, about doctors' findings. Thoreau said, "I would not have talked so much about myself if there had been anyone else I knew half as well." Sharing is healthful. But at 80-something we have learned that coping is far more productive than complaining.

One thing we have also learned is that it's perfectly all right to be angry at whatever affliction troubles us. This was hard to learn, for our generation is the one that grew up with the Great Depression and World War II, an era when we learned to "tough it out, keep our mouths shut and make the best of it." (My neighbor, Alfred, was of our generation. He collapsed while painting in his church basement. As the medics carried him out he managed to whisper hoarsely, "Put the...lid....on....the paint can.") It's been hard to accept that we can get up in the morning and say (the more loudly the better),

"I HATE this aching, I hate getting out of a warm bed, I hate the way my joints don't want to loosen up, I hate the way my little finger, which doesn't do a lick of work, still aches like a toothache just to aggravate me!" Go ahead. Improvise to suit your situation. You can do better.

But — and this is a big BUT — once having blown our stack, so to speak, we have learned to go to the next step. And that is to again speak to our ailment:

"That's it for now. I'm not wasting any more breath on you now. You're not my boss. This is my body and I'm in charge. Starting immediately, I will do all the things my doctor told me to and I will turn my own attention to living well, productively, happily and even joyfully in spite of any of your efforts to control." For some it may be a daily ritual, for others a break in a day when chronic pain, lack of mobility, diminished eyesight or hearing or any other problem has become especially nagging.

My friend Mary believes that our bodies have become so protective of our deep inner self that they will even develop physical problems to distract us so we don't have to deal with an even more painful problem — the pain lying deep within that self, that quiet place.

Which leads us to the discovery that many 80-somethings have long since made, that prayer is an effective way of coping with most problems.

Anna Palsson, 85, (not to be confused with Anna Hought, my 107-year old mentor for aging) was having radiation for pancreatic cancer. But what bothered her more was her already poor eyesight, which had worsened rather quickly over a few weeks.

"I talk to God all the time," she told her niece, "because usually there's no one else around to talk to. And then I feel so guilty and I say, 'Oh, God, forgive me for always complaining to You, You must get terribly tired of it!'"

To which her niece replied, "Oh, Anna, don't worry about that — I think God just likes to hear the sound of your voice."

Speaking with and listening to God — call it prayer, devotion, meditation — can be comforting in any painful situation. From the time of Job people have laid their concerns on what they sense are stronger, sturdier shoulders. The answer may come suddenly and miraculously. More often, the act of prayer soothes the raw edge of the problem, enabling us to look at it more clearly and to deal with it.

Ironically, the best form of prayer may be the most painful, like the pain that comes from cauterizing a wound. This is when prayer leads us to face that self in the quiet place. It is not a place we want to go alone and unarmed, and I think most 80-somethings have learned that we must enter that area surrounded by the forgiveness of God. God, who is total love and total forgiveness, creates for us an arena in which we face the old hurts, slights, injustices, pain, betrayals, and simply forgive. In doing so, we also forgive ourselves for all the oversights and shortcomings of the past 80-some years. And we accept forgiveness for what, in the words of the litany, "we have done and what we have left undone."

Remember how your mother cleaned house spring and fall?

None of this quick touch-up that's just a little better than the weekly cleaning. I remember how she washed lace curtains and I helped put them on curtain stretchers, tiny, sharp nails running the length of criss-crossed bars. We emptied the buffet, washed the good dishes and put them back. In the little bedroom upstairs that held most of the really old things, we emptied both trunks to make sure no moth had penetrated, we aired my grandmother's hand-knitted mufflers, we washed the wide-board painted floor with hot water and a little linseed oil. When we were finished, we opened all the windows and let the spring or autumn breeze blow through the house. Only a few times on a windy ocean beach have I smelled anything so gloriously fresh.

The moment of forgiveness is like that.

Forgiving ourselves and everyone else renews our energy and we begin again to cope with what I like to call "vagaries and vicissitudes," words that cover a multitude of ills. Ask most 80-somethings how they cope and they will have good answers, especially the men, the beneficent looking, rosy-cheeked men with sparse white hair and eyes that thank you for asking.

"Laughter is the best medicine," someone is sure to say. But you can't wait for someone to give you cause for laughter. You have to find it. And sometimes it comes in unlikely ways.

I went to the Hearing Clinic recently. I knew I needed hearing aids but I didn't want them and I resented taking a perfectly good morning to go across town.

An elderly man, a volunteer, was at the information desk of the building. "Can you tell me which floor the Hearing Clinic is on?"

He looked up from his newspaper. "WHAT?" he demanded. And he wasn't being funny. I chuckled over that much of the day.

Most of us laugh over our lack of memory (which, if we could only remember, we likely had even in our forties). The stories are legion. But so are the ways in which 80-somethings cope with poor memory. Here are a few:

Make lists. Not just shopping lists but a list of whom you should call tomorrow, whom you should write a note to, what chores can't wait any longer, what you really want to read.

Have a place for everything and put everything in its own place — always! Then your keys will always be there in their own china dish, the hammer won't have traveled all over the house. Divide your mail into "Take care of this this week" and "Handle this when I have time." And the place for those ball point pens that don't write any more is in the trash.

Designate your outer door as a Checkpoint Charlie: Do I have my keys, my billfold, the letters I mean to mail, my shopping list?

Victoria, a friend of my husband's family since childhood, came to visit on her way home from Fairbanks, Alaska, where she had spent the summer volunteering at a radio station. She was 85. The summer before she had smuggled Bibles into China.

She carried a briefcase and when she opened it it was full of yellow legal pads. She drew one out and picked up her pen. "Now, tell me about Irene, tell me about Angeline"— and then she broke off.

"Oh yes, I take notes! Can't rely on my memory. This way I come home and it's all there before me. Now did you know —"

Many 80-somethings find special interest groups a way not only to cope with current problems but also to prevent other problems from surfacing down the road — exercise classes, for instance, and walking tours, classes in healthful cooking and vibrant, positive spiritual groups. A group might be as specialized as fly-tying or book-binding, or have the limitless possibilities of a computer class.

On the other hand, you may choose to simply disregard your limitations and even triumph because of them. Of the French

Impressionists, several artists developed serious vision problems as well as arthritis. When Degas's eyesight began to fail in the 1890s, he turned to sculpture. Through his sixties and seventies Renoir's hands were afflicted with a crippling arthritis. But he continued to paint with a brush strapped to his wrist.

And what of Monet, did the magnificent blur of his garden canvases come about because of his blurred vision? And did his colors glow so brilliantly because of his cataract surgery in 1923?

But most would agree that the best way of coping with problems is to turn our energies into helping others.

Remember Pat, my friend in the retirement home? Pat said she had decided to adopt the Archangel Michael as her special "messenger angel."

"One day I said to him, Give me an answer to this: I have so much love and joy to give. Why am I in a place where I have no money, little freedom and no one who wants the love I offer?

"That very evening I literally ran into Maggie coming out of the elevator. I knew her when I lived along the beach; everyone who walked the beach knew Maggie. She was terse and tough but the kids all loved her. But something had happened, I think a stroke. It had brought her here and she was confused. I took her arm and I said, 'Come on, Maggie, and I'll show you the way around here.' Was that Michael at work or what?"

And then there was Kay Rose.

The first day I saw her behind the front desk of the nursing facility, she turned that quirky, glowing smile on me and said,

"When I turned 75, I decided I would call everyone my 'earth buddy.' So you are my earth buddy." From that day, as I signed in and out from my visits, we greeted each other with, "How's my earth buddy today?"

She was a small woman, dainty, with soft gray-white hair always done to perfection and a pink and white complexion that glowed like her smile. She would have moved gracefully but I sensed a certain unsteadiness when she turned quickly to answer the phone or tend to residents bringing their problems to her.

She told me she had had a stroke a few months earlier and had only recently come back to work part time. And she was coping — how she was coping!

"My hands and fingers didn't want to work any more. So I bought an old IBM Selectric typewriter and began typing on it, a finger at a time. Every time I'd hear something inspiring, or think of some encouraging saying, I'd hurry to the typewriter and type it out. I have a whole loose-leaf notebook full now!

"What I really like are thoughts that can be expressed in five words. Like, 'Love knows no artificial bounds,' or 'I can do anything better' or 'Handsome is as handsome does.' Oh, I wrote down everything! And look"— she held out her hands, nails a pale mauve, the fingers clenched and unclenched themselves. "Life is so wonderful, I can't get enough of it! I am so fortunate!"

She said her name was really Kay. "But when my mother died, I decided to 'adopt' her name and I call myself Kay Rose. It's like having her always with me." She loved roses but nasturtiums were her favorite. I told her mine had seeded themselves all over the garden.

She dealt with the steady stream of requests and complaints as she must have dealt with the stroke — calmly, cheerfully, with sweet, personal, pointed assurances. She was patient but with no hint of resignation. Her comments touched on anything that was good — the sun coming in through the west windows, a pot of mums being brought in, Mr. Harrington's springer spaniel, a peach-colored blouse, the frilly handkerchief she kept tucked under her watch band. Looking back, I'm sure that many of us who met Kay Rose remembered Anne of Green Gables and her "kindred spirit," and thought, I, too have found a kindred a spirit.

But life is not always fair, and with this, too, we have had to learn to cope. On a brilliant autumn day with the leaves just beginning to show flecks of gold, Kay Rose was walking to her hairdresser's. A mentally ill street person ran by her and shoved her so hard she hit the sidewalk and fractured her skull. She lived barely long enough to reach the hospital and then she was gone.

Hardly a day goes by but what I think of Kay Rose. And that is good. For as mystery writer P.D. James says in her *Original Sin,* "The tragedy of loss is not that we grieve but that we cease to grieve."

To which I would add, the tragedy of our impairments is not that we have them but that we are often slow learners in the art of coping.

6.

They are enormous men! The firemen come first, the station is barely eight blocks away. They are in their fire-fighting gear, heavy brown jackets, no hats, their heads looking small above the padded bodies. They seem to pour through the door, though there are only four of them. In the small, intimate circle of my living room they move as in a ballet, bears on a stage, finding their places, reaching for bags, opening cases, pulling out instruments that pick up the reading lamp's light and flash it about the room.

Larry is in his chair, his robe drawn loosely over his pajamas. His face is ashen gray, but he greets them. One brown bear kneels beside him while another pulls the robe off his shoulder and slaps a blood pressure tube on his arm. A third is taking his pulse. "What is your name? Your birth date? Have you had any heart problems before?" The fourth is on a phone. "We have an 80-year old male —"

I am not on the stage with the brown bears, and when I speak my voice sounds strange and far away in the audience. "He's in the computer in Virginia Mason Hospital, it's all there." The bear on his knees by Larry nods and smiles and turns back to Larry. "What medications are you taking?"

Now the medics arrive. There are five of them and, like late comers at a party, they try to find an open space to fit into. The firemen are gathering up their gear. There is a brief consultation and they leave. New equipment covers the floor. More questions, more blood pressure, temperature, pulse. "We're putting a tube in your throat to help you breathe. There, that wasn't so bad, was it?" Now I get the questions. Odd how clear my mind is, I am surprised.

"We're taking him to emergency — Virginia Mason, isn't it? Do you want to ride along?"

"No, don't wait. I'll call a cab." They gather up equipment, roll in the gurney. The young man who will drive him comes up to me, smiling.

"I've been here before." I frown and shake my head. "Maybe three summers ago. You had a young women at your back door at midnight and called the police."

"Oh, yes, she kept saying she was late for the wedding! I didn't dare to let her in."

"You did right. She got the help she needed. All right, we're loaded. Best way out front door or back?"

"There's a ramp off the back porch."

The young men all call out, "Goodbye!" But they wheel Larry out so quickly I cannot say goodbye, cannot kiss him. He is swathed in a yellow blanket. When they came for the girl, I remember, they wrapped her in a yellow blanket, too. I hear doors slam and gears shift. In our sleeping neighborhood they do not use the siren.

In the silence I look at Larry's clock on the mantel. It is four-thirty in the morning. It is 23 minutes since I dialed 911 and it seems like an eternity.

CHAPTER SIX

Bless My Sole

IT WAS MY FIRST VISIT. THE TALL YOUNG DOCTOR (well, aren't they all young any more?) walked into the examining room with a big grin on his face.

"So your back hurts when you brush your teeth?"

I stared at him. Then I burst out laughing. Of course! Exactly that position, bending over the sink! Or over the oven, over my shoes, or over just about anything. Wonder of wonders, I had found an orthopedic specialist who himself had a bad back!

He talked about exercise and about a regimen of half an hour lying flat and fifteen minutes of being up, repeated all day, each day for a week.

"And twice a day a half hour of walking outside. Have you ever noticed a dog when he's sick? He will struggle to get to his feet, to move. It's instinct. He knows that if he moves he will get better."

Most of us who do any serious walking at 80-something maybe found the joys of it much earlier in life and just kept walking. For others it is not too late to start. And for those who have been walkers, it's important that we not become complacent, thinking that our past walking has left us so healthy we should be able to do without it in our remaining years.

On a tour group in the Netherlands, two of our fellow travelers were the retired dean of a university medical school and his wife. His wife, 76 at the time, was always out in front of the group when we walked anywhere. But it was her husband, 78, whose statement I have long remembered.

"Each day I try to push myself a little further. If I walked a mile yesterday I will walk two miles today. If I walk a flight of stairs from one street level to another today, I'll walk it twice tomorrow. Of course," he smiled, "I couldn't do that indefinitely, but I do have to stop and jack myself up occasionally."

Health books and magazines are full of advice on the benefits of walking. Your doctor will tell you the same thing. In fact, the best place to start a program of walking is with your doctor. If there are reasons why you shouldn't attempt a regular walking plan he will know them. He will tell you what level you will benefit from and how strenuously you will want to pursue it. I boasted to my doctor once that my friend Ellen and I were trying to break our time on our daily walks along Waterfront Park. He shook his head and said with a wry smile, "Try for distance and not speed."

Your doctor may have brochures with practical tips on walking. If not, check your library or the Internet for any good magazine on health or walking. Some tips are basic. Wear comfortable clothing that does not bind or restrict movement. Choose shoes with a non-slip sole in a size that will permit you to wear athletic socks without crowding your feet. Dress for the season. Use your pockets or a fanny pack to leave your hands free for better balance.

My friend Connie has taught me always to carry a card with my name, address, phone number, emergency number, hospital preference and, if applicable, clinic number. In that pocket I add some change (for telephone or bus fare if I walk further that I planned and want a ride home) and some small bills (if I catch the aroma of cinnamon rolls from the bakery down the block from Starbucks). Sometimes I carry a pen and small notebook to jot down things I might otherwise forget. For example, last week I wanted to tell my friend Shirley, who is a cat lover, what I saw: three cats stretched out lazily on the sidewalk, evenly spaced along the block, one in the center and one near each end. Is there a cat ESP where they plan such things?

One thing the health books and walking guides never tell you, however, is that you can think as you walk.

For, let's face it, walking CAN be boring. Even if your walk takes you past a gorgeous view, your thoughts may be the same day after day: "Isn't that beautiful?" It evokes nothing more. We spend an hour or more three times a week thinking the same thoughts: This sidewalk is cracking, someone should fix it. I have to call the plumber when I get home. Wonder if Joe brought my clippers back. That man should have his muffler fixed. Is it my imagination or are playground sounds louder every year? How long have I been walking? We move our feet but not our thoughts, we stretch out legs but not our minds.

For a starter, assign yourself a topic. Start with something you heard on Public TV last night: how did Lord Francis Bacon's view of government differ from Thomas Jefferson's? Or, was the movie, *Chocolat,* a morality play on redemption? Or, how can I phrase a letter to persuade the City Council to create a park of this vacant area? Or, if I could imagine an unlikely family to live in the Dutch colonial house I just passed, what would they be like?

Some people find their walks a good time for intercessory prayer, praying for others. But there is a catch here. Often when we pray for others, God turns the prayer around as if to ask in that still small voice that may or may not be our conscience, "Is there something you could do to help?" No, intercessory prayer, I think, is best done in the mornings when we are fresh and when the prayer may lead us to reach for the phone or pick up a pen. We do not answer our own prayers, but we can purposely create a spirit in which God's answer will travel productively.

In my city walking, I "collect" gables. In the roughly three square miles within which I mainly walk, there is almost every type of house built since the turn of the century. Some, in fact, were built before 1900 and still have the original gingerbread trim in their high, peaked gables. There are the blocky, sturdy, Craftsman-style bungalows of the 1920's, some expansive two-storied homes and some so small they are like the houses one could order from the Sears Roebuck catalog in the early 1930's. There are houses without eaves, built to save on lumber during World War II. And of course, on the "view side" of the Hill, homes of the rich and famous straight from the pages of *Architectural Digest.*

Nearly all have gables. There are the peaks of the roofs, of course. But there are also gables that seem to have been added for no reason other than to enhance the house. They are like my friend Betty, who doesn't need glasses to see. But when she goes to the Opera or something like that, "I have a pair I wear to dress up my face." Some gables are nothing more than an eyebrow over a window, some shade nothing at all. Many pop out of a roof where a bedroom has been added. Some are imaginative, with a railing across the bottom to look like a balcony. Some shade fragile balconies on which I would never dare step. Some high gables rise over windows that have a shelf protruding as if to offer cookies to passing angels. I love gables.

A claustrophobic friend once said, "If I ever have to have an

MRI, I have a plan. I'm going to mentally walk through the house I was born in. I'll start at the front door and examine every room as I remember it, every piece of furniture, the pictures, the bric-a-brac, the carpets on the floor."

I decided to try it out on a day when I was walking along a familiar and somewhat uninteresting route. I started with the back door or my childhood farm home and the cement steps and the sidewalk that ran around the corner of the house to a basement door. Here was a small patch of earth between the sidewalk and the house where portulaca bloomed every summer, silky little splashes of gold and red and amber and cream. They were partly watered by the steady drip from a pipe that ran back through the wall to the drain of the icebox. My father and brothers cut the ice when it reached a thickness of 16 inches in nearby Little Lake and hauled it home in horse-drawn sleighs. It was packed in sawdust in the ice house and in summer my brothers hauled it to the house in an old wheelbarrow and carried it in with big, wicked looking ice tongs.

Besides the icebox, the back porch held all kinds of useful items that seemed to have settled into their niches long before I was born — and never moved far. My brothers' guns hung on the wall, a double-barreled and a single-barreled shotgun and a .22 gauge rifle. The shells were in the porch windowsill. It wouldn't have occurred to us then to lock them away. They came down in pheasant season and in winter for jackrabbit hunts. A crude table held seedlings in spring, cabbage and tomato, and in autumn seeds dried there — watermelon, muskmelon, zinnias, white beans, brown beans. Some years our neighbor George set up his honey-extracting spinner on the porch and extracted honey from the combs my brother Ernie, screen mask and all, took from the hives under the apple trees.

Suddenly I realized I had walked four blocks past my destination and had not even stepped across the kitchen threshold!

Many people find walking the mall to be convenient and

comfortable. It's warm in winter, the floor is level with no cracks. I have young (60-something) friends who drive to a destination to walk, in this case the three-mile trek around Green Lake. Some communities open school gyms for senior walking before school time. Walking up and down a residence corridor is good if you smile, stop to speak to people and fill your mind with grand expectations for the day.

In my area it is not unusual to see very old people walking to and from the supermarket or the drug store, some with canes, most with a cloth shopping bag, all of them watching carefully as they step on and off curbs. Some are well into their nineties — what a testimonial to walking! If they had depended on wheels, would they be walking now?

I was sorry when Dr. Cahn moved his office from our neighborhood. Not only was he within walking distance, but he was a storyteller. He said I reminded him of his Uncle Benny because I tend to "tough things out." He told how his Uncle Benny called his doctor one day.

"Doc, I think I've got a little pain."

The doctor responded, "Meet me in the emergency room in 15 minutes." Then the doctor called the hospital. "Get ready for something big."

It was true. Benny had a ruptured appendix.

But Dr. Cahn also had a story about people who keep walking.

He grew up in a Chicago neighborhood next to a big Italian section. A group of doctors had set up a clinic in the Italian section and it was doing so well they decided to add another specialist. So they went to the residents and asked what they wanted — an orthopedic surgeon, a cardiovascular specialist, maybe a psychiatrist? The spokesman for those assembled, mostly retired, asked if they could discuss it and give their answer in a week. When they came back in a week they said they wanted a foot doctor.

"A foot doctor?" The clinic spokesman frowned.

"Yes, sir." All nodded assent. "You see, you can have those other things and still get around. But when your feet give out and you can't walk to the tavern and see your friends, it's no good."

They got a foot doctor.

7.

It wasn't Larry's first experience with Seattle's 911 team nor would it be the last. There had been earlier calls, one on a hot summer day when he was walking to his apartment from the post office and the angina had set in. He had taken his three nitroglycerines but there had been no place to sit down so he tried to reach the apartment building. Instead he collapsed against a utility pole. The young woman who found him and called 911 stayed with him, comforting and encouraging him, until the aid car came. Even in his pain and exhaustion he made sure he had her name and when he found her in the phone book he sent her flowers.

Nor was it his last stay in the hospital. They could do no more bypasses. They added a stent to open an artery and increase blood flow. Medication was changed, added, taken away.

But he always bounded back, optimistic, full of all the life he could muster. We celebrated our October birthdays a second time and then a third. For all that we were well into our eighties now, we lived as though we had unlimited time. "When they get my heart stabilized," he'd say, "then we'll make that trip back East to see all my family." Or, "There's a lovely hotel in Ketchikan, overlooks the city and the harbor, and it's only an hour and a half flight. Maybe this summer."

In the meantime, we settled into the comfortable routine of a couple who might have known each other for years. Which was strange, for I soon realized we had come from two very different marriages.

After his years at sea and after retirement from a position that absorbed much of his time, it seemed that he and his wife had done everything together, even grocery shopping, even small errands. So it was natural for him to say,

"Let's go out to Molback's and see their big poinsettia tree," or, "Get your coat, I'm taking you out to lunch," or, "I need batteries, let's go to Bartell's and we can look for birthday cards," or, "Tomorrow's the Pearl Harbor Survivors breakfast, you're going with me, aren't you?"

My marriage had been good but with many separate interests. And after many years alone, I wasn't prepared for this.

"Larry," I said at last, "you need to find things to do on your own. And I need a little time of my own. Why don't you try the Brown Bag group at the church on Tuesdays? Or take a friend to lunch instead of me?"

And he did and it was a revelation to me. For instead of doing all the things I had planned for my time alone, I found myself walking around the silent house waiting for him to come home.

But we settled into a comfortable pattern. Every morning as I cooked oatmeal with raisins he brought me my vitamins for the day. He wrote dates on batteries and put them in things, he read the manual for the washer and told me what was wrong with it. He read parts of the evening paper to me. I cleaned the yard in fall and planted flowers in spring, he marked two dates on the calendar, the spring and fall equinoxes: "Call window washers."

And every morning and evening we told each other, "I love you with all my heart."

Even when he complained of not feeling well one day ("No, don't call the doctor, I see my cardiologist Thursday, he'll give me something,"), even when he had difficulty walking that Thursday and we needed a wheel chair to reach the cardiologist's office, even then I thought we had years ahead. Something this good, I thought, must last a long, long time.

CHAPTER SEVEN

Mixed Messages

IN ARCHBISHOP HUNTHAUSEN'S POEM, MENTIONED
earlier, these lines are found:

> "Children are not too sophisticated
>   to wonder
>   to talk of their shoes
>   to reach out
>   and up
>   and all around
>   for that's where miracles are."

When we have passed 80 years we know pretty much where the
miracles are. And we know we must reach out, and up, and all
around, to touch them. But it's not easy because there are so many
mixed messages reaching us from all sides.

Not everyone is as clear headed and to the point as my no-
nonsense friend Connie (of the squirrel caper). She has a saying:

"If you're old and you think old, then you ARE old. But if you're old and you think young, you're STILL old."

Instead we are barraged by the media with all kinds of promises that we can do anything we set our minds to: we can play basketball with our grandchildren, we can climb mountain trails, we can kayak in the San Juan Islands, we can teach a college class in our specialty. All worthy goals and attainable by some — remember the retired medical school dean who pushed himself a little further each day? And my friend May, the camel rider; only a painful leg kept her from making another trip to Israel at 88. But for others who may have that painful leg, or a limiting heart or the effects of a stroke, those admonitions are themselves painful.

Part of the problem lies in the aging of the Baby Boomers. They are creeping past that magical number of 55, when the word "senior" begins to be heard. There are so many of them and their buying power is so immense that media attention to "seniors" is now more and more focused on them. Magazine articles on aging use 50-year old models; the women have wrinkle-free skin, the men have hair. We read the articles and look at the pictures and we are made to feel guilty because we are not reaching the potential we are supposed to be achieving.

At the same time, we are receiving messages of a totally different kind. Most come from our own bodies: diminished eyesight, arthritic pain, a faulty heart, radiation and chemo, the varied effects of strokes and falls and fractures. I met my friend Jean, then 84, when she was in a healthcare, being treated after a bad fall. She and her husband, 95, had been turning a mattress when it flipped, hurling Jean to the floor. "The last thing I remember saying was, 'You can let go, honey, I've got hold of it'." In her heavy body brace, she was tooling around in her wheel chair, making sketches of patients and staff alike. My friend Ruth, 78, is an avid sailor and was helping friends ready their boat for winter when she missed the bottom rung of a ladder. She broke her hip.

Some of the messages come from family and friends. Be careful. Can you see the curb? Take my hand. It's too far. It's not safe. You're getting tired. Are you taking your medications? Are you sure? And this wonderful question from my 60-something friend Tom, "You look good. How old do you tell people you are these days?"

Sometimes we appreciate the concern, other times we resent it. The woman stocking shelves in the supermarket tells me, "The garbanzo beans are in the next aisle, dear." Why does it annoy me to be called "dear" by a perfect stranger? Why can't I say, "I'm sorry but I find it demeaning. You are giving me a message that I am old and therefore to be treated as some sort of developmentally disabled child."

So how do 80-somethings handle these mixed messages? In the way that 80 years have taught us to handle most things: by balance.

We stretch and reach as far as we can — up and out and all around. But when physical ailments or other circumstances prevent that, when we feel captive to our limitations, when we have "hung our harps on the poplar trees," we turn inward. And therein lies the greatest adventure of all.

"There is," wrote Elizabeth Cady Stanton, "a solitude within us — a solitude called self." And in that self lies the power to go beyond purely physical activities into a world that is without limits or boundaries, a world of realizations and imagination. And sometimes the path to that solitude leads through circumstances we would not choose.

Macular degeneration keeps me from seeing details plainly. But James Thurber, the ebullient author and cartoonist best known for his drawings in The New Yorker, became totally blind in later years and he said, "Imagination does not become blind," and, "Some people are handicapped by seeing." In other words, the things we take in by seeing may distance us from the panorama of imagination.

Various illnesses make the prospect of a plane trip too unpleasant, the crowding, the delays, the blurred departure screens, the frantic transfers. Ah, but the libraries and TV channels are full of travel films, viewed from the comfort of your own chair, your own cup of tea beside you, no waiting for the flight attendants to drag the cart down the long aisle.

And what about your own videos and travel albums, the photo records you said were for your "rocking chair years?" Bring them out of the storeroom and spread them on the table! Remember how you felt when you first saw St.Peter's in Rome, be surprised that the spring colors of Kuekenhof Gardens are still bright. Invite a friend to see your 1997 Alaska fishing trip and encourage him to bring his own album or video. Ask your library for a tape of Frances Mayes's *Under the Tuscan Sun* and play it while you turn your album pages through your first trip to northern Italy.

If you have kept journals through the years, and if the entries have become more brief and sketchy, bring them out! Read the passages that you wrote when you felt strongly about something or someone. Thomas Merton once wrote,

"When you read your journal, you find out that your latest discovery is something you already found out about five years ago. Still, it is true that one penetrates deeper and deeper into the same idea and the same experience."

We minimalize. We find joy in smaller and simpler things. Theodor Kittelsen was a 19th century Norwegian artist and writer who spent most of his life in abject poverty. His greatest contribution was setting down the old folk tales of trolls and nisser and hulder and other terrifying creatures, a sort of Peter Grimm of the North. One day, looking around his home, he wrote,

"I was suddenly aware of such a sweet and beneficent connection with Nature, in the pattern of the drapes, and in every sight and sound around my house, an infinite and unaccountable friendliness all at once, like an atmosphere sustaining me."

Interestingly, there is a means by which we can, at the same time, be very still by ourselves and yet reach up and out and beyond. It is the computer and the Internet, and 80-somethings are not too old to use and enjoys its means of communicating.

If you are not familiar with the world of computers and e-mail, I would urge you to consider it. If your vision is good enough to read the screen and if your fingers can tap out words, no matter how slowly, you can reach out into the whole world!

Ask a young relative or friend, possibly a child, to show you the simple basics to get you started: how to turn on the computer, how to write a brief message, how to send it across the country or across the world, how to receive a message and how to turn the computer off. You are on your way! Manuals are written for anyone who can read simple directions and follow cartoon-like procedures. You don't need to know the inner workings. Many libraries and senior centers have computer classes for seniors. At first you may only want to send notes to grandchildren or distant friends without having to look for an envelope and stamp. As you progress, you research the world — the art treasures of the Vatican, Burmese elephants pulling logs, chefs in the south of France, information on the area where your grandparents were born.

But even a pen is a tool for giving voice to your imagination. Initiate correspondence with friends who have retired in other areas. Find distant relatives and offer to exchange information on the family tree. Write an intimate story of your childhood years and it will live among your family long after you are gone. If you already correspond with friends and family, let yourself go beyond "I am fine, hope all is well with you."

My friend Jan (pronounced "Yon") wrote to say his grandmother in Sweden had just turned 100. He went on to tell how her husband had contracted tuberculosis at a very young age and could not work.

"They were very poor but with a cow and some chickens managed to survive. Then the young husband died. They laid him out on the kitchen table. When the undertaker came, he was about to take the cow for his services but my grandmother chased him out of the yard with a broom."

Write a short poem and send it to a friend. My cousin John always carries two or three of his own poems in a pocket. He will read them for you, all you have to do is ask. Sometimes he sends me one. He may describe a Minnesota winter, ice fishing, his love for his sister, springtime. Be as imaginative as a child!

One spring day when the sun was warm and the trees had that pale lime-green look of April, my friend Louise and I took the No. 3 bus to the ferry terminal and boarded a ferry to Bainbridge Island. We had lunch, strolled through Winslow's shops and returned as the sun was nearing the Olympic peaks to the west. A few days later Louise sent me this:

DIFFERENT BUS ROUTE

It started when I got off the ferry
A feeling of alarm
That the shops seen as we hurried to board
Now seemed in the twilight gloom
Different
Menacing

My friend, older than I
With eyesight failing
So that she marks bus stops

By historic large buildings
Rather than street signs
Which she can't read
My friend led the way unerringly
Across intersections
To the proper bus shelter

I trailed
Walked exactly where she walked
Stood exactly beside her in the queue
As if placing my feet
In deep snow footprints
Afraid to step out into drifts
And be swallowed up
In deathly whiteness

The bus came and we rode
Conversation around us
Of calm everyday things
Landmarks around us
Which I should have known
I have lived here fifty years
Leafy trees flashing by
But not trees I recognized
Not the trees I know by heart
On my daily walks
She paid on getting out
I had my money ready
And I paid

My car was at the bus stop
We drove to the supermarket
My car and I
I took the cart down the aisles
And picked every needed item

From its accustomed place
Thinking of tomorrow's menu
Getting out my checkbook
Pushing aside the knowledge
That like my father and grandmother
Before me
I will be the one
With the bright ribbon on my door
I will be the one
In the nursing home
Following the yellow line
To find my way

And I wrote back:

No, my friend, it will not be your door
With the tulip-bordered plaque saying,
    "LOUISE. WELCOME."

You will be at the door of the activity room:
"Watercolor to the left, clay sculpturing right.
Charlotte, how lovely you look! You should wear
    blue always.
Arthur, you look positively British
In your tweed vest. Don't spill paint on it.
And have you signed my petition over here?
Hmmm? William, what a nice thing to say!
Won't you sit at my table at dinner?"

The No.3 bus route is my lifeline.
I know the gargoyled old buildings by their faces.
In the Federal Building an elevator will take you to
    the next level,
And the outdoor escalator up the next hill.
There are stairways

Down which I will not go again.
I will show you short cuts
Any time you ask.

Your yellow line is dedication and devotion, action and
Follow-up, informed advocacy, unflagging care.

You must continue to walk it with us
Even when we do not ask.

8.

A girl with long, straight yellow hair sits cross-legged on the floor in front of Room 207, writing on a yellow pad. She looks up at the tall, thin young man leaning against the doorframe.

"How shall I say this?" she asks. "Shall I say, 'loving mother of four, grandmother of five?'"

People come here to die. Oh, not all — some come for rehab and some live out several years of their lives here. It is light and pleasant. It has a good smell. The nurses and aides are cheerful and efficient and, except for some weekenders from the Agency, are seldom cross. Sometimes I forget that people come here to die.

"You're really quite ill," the cardiologist said, "Your heart has finally become so fragile there is no other procedure we can do. We will help you find a good place for end-time care." Not "terminal." "End-time" is just as flat and cruel and final but it is somehow easier to say. I insist I shall take him home but his children and my children say no, it is too much, you have been through this once.

Blessedly, this place has a bed open. It is a six-minute drive from my home. I can almost walk it. Numbly we settle in. Larry has a big window on his side of the room. Bob is on the other side of the curtain. Bob is an old Navy man, too, but hard of hearing. There is a bathroom, and a sink in the room where Bob's teeth have taken up permanent residence. Larry complains about nothing. As he has always done with waiters and bank tellers, he remembers the names of all who wait on him.

I come every day, I tape the colorful greeting cards on the wall, the children's hand-made cards. Sometimes he says, "I don't see why I can't come home," and sometimes, "This is a good place to be." We hold hands, we laugh, we say our prayer, we talk freely of death and

81

the life beyond. I tell him about my father-in-law and the angel. He smiles. The first weeks are almost good.

But a change begins. Taking a cue from the heart, other parts of the body fail. Edema sets in, his legs swell. Medication is changed, added. The old Larry is slipping away. In his place is someone increasingly taut, frightened, anxious, afraid to be alone. He sits in his wheel chair until he is exhausted, but as soon as he is helped to bed he must get up again. I stay later into the evening. The pastor sits with him. "No, no, I'm not afraid of dying," he repeats, "but what's happening to me? This is not me!" We try to reason with him — weakness, illness — and we pray. But always so frantic.

His sons come and go and come again. He rallies his energy to be hospitable. They reassure him. Hospice people come. They are comforting and encouraging but nothing changes. They explain to him and to us what the medicines are supposed to be accomplishing. Nothing changes. Ai, the little Korean nurse, throws her arms around him and says, "Larry, Larry, everything is going to be all right!"

He loses interest in food. He begins to sleep more. Thank God he is not struggling to be up! I am happy when Craig is on duty nights. Craig is his favorite nurse. I talk a bit with Bob when I leave. Bob says, "It will be all right, dear."

It is eleven at night when Craig calls. Oh, God, Craig was with him, dear, kind Craig! "It went quickly, sooner than we thought. I saw something was wrong and ran to get extra pain medication, then I held him and said goodbye to him and told him the time had come to meet Edythe and all the others, and then he was gone."

CHAPTER EIGHT

The Priest Who Walked Through the Window

OLD HOUSES HAVE THEIR OWN SOUNDS. BUILT IN 1924, mine has survived three moderately strong earthquakes and a number of lesser rumbles. The old beams are as sound as ever, but there are creaks and sharp cracks, especially in the stairwell and especially when outside temperatures are changing. There are knocks, like spirits rapping. On windy nights the fireplace moans and whistles behind its glass doors. An east wind at night reminds me the cedar has grown too close to my bedroom window, it rasps and thrashes at the panes.

At night, the noises are always at night. Even in summer when the weather is good and the windows open, I hear the intermittent rustling in the snowball bushes next door and I know the raccoons are back. Their domain is a huge, overgrown ravine that slices through the east side of our hill, and on summer nights they fan out to forage for foods the ravine doesn't provide.

Or is it the raccoons? Is it the wind? You know the feeling. You come awake and quickly, before your daytime self emerges, you begin your litany, "All I want is to go back to sleep, all I want is to go —" But it doesn't work. The clock says three-thirty. You are as awake as you would be at seven — or more so!

Some people find this a good time to talk to God. Or, more importantly, to listen to God. But it's too easy for the mind to wander and to dwell on wants rather than praise. Conversations with God, I think, are best carried out at the kitchen sink, or while walking, or weeding, or when one is early at church and sitting alone.

When she couldn't sleep, my sister-in-law, Vinie, would name all her relatives, extending as far out on the family tree as she could reach. She didn't think of it as prayer but I think it had the same effect. Her warm and loving interest in every cousin and in-law shone through her conversation and touched us. We knew we were under an umbrella of caring.

So, I've taken a page from her book. When I can't sleep, I think about people. I pan my mental camera over the years and pick a face here or there to focus on.

For example, I think about Elmer. In the winter of 1930, when I was 13, Elmer came to work on our farm for a few months. He was a relative of a relative, a string bean of a man with piercing blue eyes, a black pompadour that kept falling over his forehead and the brown skin of people whose forebears came from the very north of Sweden. On a farm in winter there are only the daily chores to do, no seeding or cultivating or harvesting, and only now have I realized he came because he had no other place to go.

But Elmer more than earned his keep. That winter we barely listened to Radio WNAX in Yankton, South Dakota, or to WLS in Chicago, neither with the earphones nor the trumpet-shaped loud speaker. That winter, supper over, the dishes washed, my homework done and the men in from milking and washed up, we settled into the warm kitchen — my father, my mother (still fussing with kitchen chores), my two grown brothers and myself. Elmer liked to sit on the floor, hunkered up against the tall radiator that had mittens drying on its top.

And then the stories would begin. Elmer knew the history of the area, going back for as many generations as it had been settled. He knew how the families were intertwined. He knew the small tragedies and the larger than life characters. He had literally lived among the Polish and Bohemian immigrants who farmed just south of our all-Scandinavian ghetto and he knew their foods and traditions — and their sorrows.

Elmer loved the sound of words. Once he and a friend traveled to Okeechobee, Florida, so that Elmer could see a town whose name rolled so melodiously off the tongue. He went to Oskaloosa, Iowa, for the same reason. The winter before he came to us he had gone to Tillamook, Oregon, and had milked cows on an ocean side dairy farm for three months.

"Oh, how it rained, how it rained!" He drew out the word. We could see the barnyard flooding, hear the torrent coming down as he ran between the house and barn.

Years later, Tom Robbins would write of rain in *Another Roadside Attraction,* "And it rained a fever. And it rained a silence. And it rained sorceries and the saturnine eye of the totem."

Elmer's rain stories were even more evocative, more alliterative. The accent was Swedish but I wondered sometimes if a leprechaun had not dropped a blarneyed changeling into that family.

I think of Elmer now and of my adolescent hunger for new places, even Oskaloosa. I pay him tribute as I shop my local supermarket and buy Tillamook cheddar and Tillamook Brown Cow ice cream.

Sometimes I think about Anna Hought, my mentor for growing old, my inspiration, my friend. Anna came as a young woman from Norway to homestead on the bleak, windswept prairies of northern Montana. For three years she "proved up" her land, living in a shack that had been abandoned by a sheepherder years before. When she married a young farmer just back from service in World War I, things weren't much better those first years.

But Anna was full of upbeat stories about life on the prairie. When we plied her with questions about the hardships, the isolation, she would shrug as if it weren't important and say, "I always tried to make things nice."

There was the winter when the only meat they'd had for weeks was fat pork that had been salted down in a large crock and was growing rancid. It was too cold and too far to walk to town and, anyway, the money wouldn't have reached for meat.

One frigid morning they saw a movement in their yard. It was an antelope.

"Oh, she was so beautiful! She looked toward the house and then — oh, she was so dainty! — she walked around the side of the house. I heard Ed go upstairs, take his shotgun off the wall. I heard the door open. I prayed, O God, don't let him shoot that beautiful animal! And then in the next breath I prayed, O God, let him hit the animal so we can have meat!" She heard two shots.

Ed skinned and dressed out the antelope and that afternoon they roasted one hindquarter.

"That night," Anna went on, "I woke up and all I could think of was the meat. The moon made the house light. I went down to the kitchen and cut myself a slice from the cold roast. Then I heard Ed come down, and we stood there in the cold kitchen eating cold leftover antelope and thanking God for our good fortune."

When Anna died at 107, I said to her daughter Nora, "I think this is what Anna would have wanted now."

"I don't know," Nora replied thoughtfully. "She was having so much fun in the nursing home."

Many times I think about Randall. I can still see him striding down the center aisle of our church, the big stained glass window in back casting a sort of glow on the scarlet robe that seemed to fan out behind him. He was in his late thirties but looked younger, lithe, black-haired, intense, with a face that was by turns jubilant or stricken.

We were a staid congregation ten years ago, accustomed to white robe or black robe, suspicious of theatricals and sudden movements. And his assignment was only for a year as an interim pastor, a fill-in, while we went through the process of calling one to replace the newly retired shepherd of our flock. What right did he have to be so — so different?

But from the first Randall shared his passion with us. It was a passion for justice, for living the life rather than talking the talk, for loving the unlovely, for worshipping God with joy and splendor while walking in the humble and healing steps of His Son.

His growing up had been in an area only some sixty miles away but so rural it seemed to us like a different time. The cornfields came almost to the door of the church that was the center of his childhood. We laughed at his warm and funny stories but we began to see ourselves in them.

The year he was eleven several of his boy cousins came, as they always did, to spend part of the summer on the farm. On one particular Sunday afternoon Randall's parents left to visit relatives nearby, charging the boys not to "turn on the stove or tear up the house."

In the middle of their roughhousing, one of the boys spotted an old black car slowly making its way up the long drive to the house. When it reached the farmyard, two elderly women dressed in navy blue and clutching their purses climbed painfully out.

"It's the Jehovah's Witnesses," hissed Randall from the lookout window. "Let Gary go to the door. He's Catholic, and they won't bother you if you're Catholic."

Somewhat nervously Gary took up his position at the door while the others hid in the kitchen. He made short work of his task and the two women made their slow and measured walk back to the car and down the long drive.

A half hour later the phone rang. "Randall?" It was his mother. "What in the world is going on up there? Your two great-aunts came to pay a call and they tell us a boy came to the door and said, 'We're Catholic and we don't want any,' and slammed the door!"

It was only a year. But he taught us to stretch our love far beyond anything we had dreamed we could. And in doing so we came to love each other with a free and undemanding love.

Two years after he left us, Randall died at Bailey Bouché House, a hospice for AIDS patient. He left us six glorious angel banners he had stitched himself — and much, much more.

❧

Edith would have fit to a T anyone's description of a maiden aunt. She was the sister of my aunt by marriage and when I was a child she came twice a year to spend a week or two on the farm with us. In the summer she came during the busy season in the house, when canning fruits and vegetables came at the same time as feeding threshing crews. Edith didn't help all that much; she suffered from various mysterious ailments, you might say she was frail in a sturdy sort of way. She would sit in the shade of the box elder trees and shell the peas my mother had picked earlier and would can later. She was slight of build with wispy hair she managed to contain in a knot at the nape of her neck. She was given to long sighs but she also had the most melodious laugh I had ever heard. My father loved to tease her. I think he did it to hear her laugh. My mother's laugh was more grudging, or apologetic, as if she felt she should not be so frivolous.

The best time was when Edith came after Christmas, ostensibly to help my mother cut carpet rags that would later be woven into "runners" for the house. Now the radiator was turned on in the parlor, a room usually closed off in winter to save heat. The Christmas tree and decorations were still up. Edith would sit on the three-legged revolving stool in front of the reed organ, playing and singing in her lovely soprano.

She sang them all, one after the other: "The Last Rose of Summer," "The Old Oaken Bucket," "Just a Song at Twilight," "Old Black Joe," "When You and I Were Young, Maggie." She sang hymns, "Bringing In The Sheaves," "Just As I Am," "He Leadeth Me," "Sweet Hour of Prayer."

But she brought more than music, she brought tales from the village that didn't reach us even on the 8-party telephone line. I think there were hours at home when she would sit with her crocheting by the parlor heater with isinglass windows, the coals glowing red. Contemporaries of her aged parents would drop in, old crones with raveled sweaters, one over the other, and they would recall tales of their generation and the one before that. Edith had her own sweep of history.

"Oh, the stories I would tell you if I only could!" She would exclaim, her eyes sparkling with mischief. But sometimes she would put on the face she wore when she sang in the Baptist choir and say soberly, "Well, they are all gone now so perhaps we can speak of them." At times like that I would be sent off on an errand.

I wonder now what unfulfilled dreams drifted through the songs and stories. Her voice was so beautiful, so crystalline pure. Had she ever dreamed of singing in a great concert hall, or even in a church as big as our whole farmyard? I doubt if her aged parents, had they even had the means, would have let her go alone to the city to study and work. Had she dreamed of marrying and having children? Perhaps marrying a Baptist minister and being allowed to conduct the choir and sing her own solos?

Or was she like the maiden aunt in Whittier's "Snowbound," who had put her unfulfilled dreams aside and sat, mostly unnoticed, in a corner with her knitting?

I think of Edith now, of her unfulfilled dreams, of all our unfulfilled dreams. Were they so bad after all?

ও

Unlike Edith, Wally's Aunt Tillie was probably not the aunt we find in most of our old photo albums, the one with a neckline a little higher than anyone else's, the one with the sensible shoes, the slight smile, the air of competence and infallibility. No, that would not be Tillie. Why do I think about her? Because right now, 60 and 70 years after those Fourth of July parades, I'm sure Wally and I are the only ones who ever give his Aunt Tillie a thought. She deserves a thought.

Wally is my neighbor and my friend, five years my junior. Over coffee Wally has told me wonderful stories, terrifying stories, of growing up in the trackless wilderness of the border lakes between Minnesota and Canada. His father was a guide for fishing parties, his mother a member of the Chippewa tribe. Because they lived sometimes on the Canada side and sometimes on the U.S. side ("There was no fence, you didn't always know where you were"), there were disputes over where he should go to school. Most years he was sent to board with one family or another through the school year. "None of them really wanted me but in the 1930s they really wanted that $20 a month."

There was one Christmas vacation when he was brought part way home by a logger who lived in the area. The logger stopped his Model T pickup at the shore of the lake that lay between Wally and home. The lake had barely frozen over and would not yet bear the weight of a car. The logger unloaded a homemade sled and tossed a 100-pound sack of potatoes on it. He pulled the sled to the edge of the lake and handed Wally the rope.

"Be careful with the potatoes," he told Wally, who was all of eight. "Your pa sent word they're about out. Now just go, they're watching for you on the other side."

But lake ice creates sound as it settles in. Halfway across, Wally heard the moaning and grinding rise to a crescendo. Terrified, he dropped the sled rope and raced for the other side, his heart hammering, his breath coming in gasps.

"My father was mad about the potatoes because he had to go out on the lake and get them in a hurry before they froze," Wally recalls now. "But my mother was glad to see me."

For all the uncertainties of his childhood, Wally knew his parents loved him. "They never got drunk over Christmas. New Years, now, that was a real humdinger. But Christmas belonged to me." He tells of going to work in the mines when he was 13 and drinking along with the men. Wally has taught me much over the years and much has come from his AA book and the 12 Steps.

Wally's Aunt Tillie? Oh, yes. Whenever he and his family could make the trip to town, Aunt Tillie was always there for them. I think there was an uncle somebody, too, but he was far in the past. And for Aunt Tillie, the greatest holiday of the year was the Fourth of July, for the big parade passed right by her second floor apartment window!

"By the time they started hanging the red, white and blue bunting over the street, Aunt Tillie would have her outfit all ready — a new white dress, white pumps, white purse, white gloves. She'd have a perm at Esther's Beauty Shoppe.

"The town band was a big deal then, white uniforms with gold braid all over them. The loggers all came in from the woods and the town was jumping. Everyone waited for the parade.

"Trouble was, the loggers all came in three, four days early and the partying began. By the morning of the Fourth Aunt Tillie would be watching the parade from her upstairs window on Main Street. She'd be in her old faded pink bathrobe, the white dress hung over a chair and the white pumps under the bed. Aunt Tillie would have the world's worst hangover and it about killed her when the band stopped in front of her building and somebody hit the cymbals with a crash."

Wally's stories about his Aunt Tillie always end on the same note. "No matter what she was like, I always knew she loved me. She had a heart as big as the whole outdoors and she loved me, I knew that."

❧

And sometimes the priest comes to mind, the one who walked through the window. Well, he didn't actually walk through it. But when he left my crowded little office in the community newspaper building he mistook the plate glass window for the swinging glass door and walked right into it. "I'm all right, I'm all right," he kept protesting.

He was a missionary priest who had been serving in Honduras and Guatemala. He had come to drop off an announcement of a preaching mission he was holding at nearby Sacred Heart Church. "Tell me more about your work," I said, "and we'll do a longer story." We talked for an hour.

Then, maybe because he had found a willing non-Catholic listener, he said hesitantly, "I have a theory but it's not what you might call theologically acceptable."

"May I quote you? I asked.

He smiled. "Maybe better not. But I believe there is a great pool of grace that surrounds the earth. And every time we say a Mass or light a candle or breathe a prayer or help someone or say a kind word, we add to that pool.

"And when we need comfort or encouragement or any other kind of blessing, we draw from that pool. It never runs dry."

The story has stayed with me over 25 years. I draw from that pool of grace daily and when I can I add to it. Sometimes it makes me thing of preacher Jim Casey in Steinbeck's *Grapes of Wrath*, who thought maybe all people had "one big soul that everybody's part of."

I think of them all, God's children like myself, created in His image, threads of color in the fabric I call my life.

9.

I am readying the garden for winter. I have cut the dahlia stalks down and mounded earth over the scarred remains, hoping frost won't reach the tubers this winter. I have pulled up the ragged annuals. The hosta is still green and can wait for the first frost, then it will die and be disposed of. I have dumped basket after basket of soggy vegetation into the compost bin.

I work mechanically, dully. I feel the chill of late autumn. Sometimes, straightening, stretching, I look toward the house. There is no angel on the roof. I am afraid to go in, it is so empty, so changed.

Why does this heavy, gray sadness permeate everything like a fog? Grief, yes, that I had expected. Loneliness, of course. Comfort there had been plenty of — a church filled with friends to tell him goodbye, our families so wonderfully kind, the little surprises, the unexpected notes. But this sadness that touches even things that had nothing to do with Larry? I wait for the No.3 bus and when it rounds the corner tears well up. He never rode the No.3, for God's sake!

But as I smooth the dirt and spread fertilizer over the spots where bulbs will peep through in February, I think I am beginning to understand. It has to do with tidying up. It has to do with this smooth, black area and its readiness for spring. It has to do with my compulsions to bring things to a proper closing.

This last chapter of our lives had been so perfect I had expected it would have a storybook ending. A storybook death, with all of us gathered around him, holding him, saying goodbye, waiting for one more word, perhaps, "Keep smiling!" Maybe a last Irish grin.

But it came too quickly. We were not there. He died with only Craig to tell him goodbye, dear, wonderful Craig whose voice broke on the phone and who cried with me when I came.

And those last weeks with the restlessness and panic, so unlike that positive person of unshakable faith — why couldn't we help him? Why couldn't we reach him?

I put the garden tools in the shed and close the door. Dusk is closing in, coming early now. I hear an unmistakable sound. The Canada geese are flying south, the city lights have confused them. God, help them find their way. Thank you that I heard them. Thank you for all the small joys even when the world is gray.

CHAPTER NINE

Lost and Found

"NOTHING MUCH HAS HAPPENED AROUND HERE," wrote Ray in his Christmas letter, "but we have been going to far too many funerals."

Yes, the eighties are a time of many losses and the loss of loved ones is, of course, the most devastating of all. But these losses occurred when we were 70-something and in all the years before. The difference is that in our 80s we are better at dealing with loss. The pain is as great, the tears as close to the surface, but we are better equipped and we have honed our skills through experience.

For all the help that Hospice and grief counseling classes have given many of us, we have learned that there is one step that only we can take. Before any healing can begin, we need to face directly into the pain, to walk straight into the finality of death. There is no going back. It is irreversible. Eighty-year olds have learned at last to say, "I accept this. I am devastated by it, I may be angry. But it is a fact of life and I accept that and I am ready now to deal with it."

If we could get rid of some of the euphemisms it would help. Let's face it: no matter how strong our belief in life after death may be, we see the end of the physical body. Our loved one did not "pass away" or "pass on." He died, she died. Like this season's leaves, people die. It's as simple as that. Why is it so hard to speak the word?

On the morning of my husband's memorial service, my brother's wife died. Carl called to tell me. He was 80 then, I was not yet 70. He said the best thing he could ever have said to me: "Well, Florence, this is how it is now."

Once having acknowledged the finality, the grieving process — and the healing — can begin. At eighty, we have learned the importance of being in touch with our own self. My friend Marion insisted on driving herself to her husband's committal service in the cemetery. "But what will people think?" demanded her grandson, riding beside her. "I don't know," she replied, "but it's something I have to do." We have also recognized the importance of caring for our own health, of making time for rest. We acknowledge the need to have time alone. We focus on spiritual strength and the promises we believe. We set goals and try to avoid stress as much as possible.

Marion believes grief is like a mountain. "You have to climb it and get over it and each of us does it by his or her own climbing trail."

But some people, having reached the top, make the mistake of stopping, of not going on to explore the other side. They fail to see that the same azure sky stretches over this side. In their belief that the other side is barren, they fail to see pockets of wildflowers, Indian paintbrush and wild poppies. They refuse to look for new trails that will take them past fresh and wonderful vistas. They spend too much time stretching to look back to the point where they started their climb. They become frozen in time, afraid to let go of "that empty chair."

"I decided that chair could be used for something else," says Marion. She has a small room off her kitchen where her everyday world is centered. Here she phones friends, writes letters, handles accounts, keeps her appointment book, knits and watches TV. Both their leather chairs are there, hers and Chuck's. But on his, she keeps close at hand papers she's working on, letters to be answered, bills to be paid, shopping list, the menu for next week's luncheon. (She has been active in her college sorority for 60-some years.)

But there are other kinds of losses. Earlier we talked about learning to cope with loss of vision, of mobility, of memory, of our long-established patterns of living.

For many, one of the keenest losses is giving up driving. You may have decided on your own that it was time, or your children may have hinted at it long enough. You may, God forbid, have had a judge take it out of your hands. You may have had a family member take your car, ostensibly "to fix that knock," only to discover that yes, you could do without it.

But it is a loss of independence, of convenience, of a whole way of life. We are the generation that goes back to the glory days of the Model T Ford, the Model A, the V-8, the Chevy roadster with a rumble seat, the Essex, the Grant, the Hupmobile and all the other beauties. When we tell each other, "That was a very good year," we're not talking about wine. Our hands are most at home on the steering wheel. Our right arm may have numerous aches but they disappear when we reach to put the key in the ignition.

But we survive. The same year that severely arthritic feet forced my brother Carl to give up walking to the post office every day, macular degeneration forced him to give up driving. But he had a riding mower for his yard and he was able to weed and water the flower bed that lay along the sidewalk. His conversation those years was peppered with stories about the people who passed the garden and stopped to chat.

"One neighbor came by and wanted to know what all the blue flowers were. I told him they were phlox. He said I should put a light over them. When I asked him why I should do that he said, 'So you could watch your phlox by night.'"

People living in the country and in small towns may drive to a later age than those of us in big cities. On the other hand, those in cities with a good transit system are less affected by the loss of our cars. In the 25 years we were neighbors, Boyd and Ella never owned a car. Public transit and an occasional taxi took them anywhere they wanted to go. Upon retiring, Boyd spent two years riding the Seattle Metro buses to their furthest points. He rode to Black Diamond of the early coal mines and checked out the bakery. He rode to Carnation to see farmland, to Snoqualmie Falls for a hamburger. Once my neighbor Lori mapped out a route by which we could reach the ocean, a hundred miles away, all by local public transit systems. We never had the courage to try it.

One loss that is more common to this decade than another age is the loss of identity.

"I can understand why no one asks my opinion any more," observed one friend in her middle 80s. "But I don't like the way they look through me as if I'm not there." Another said, "When I was able to go to all the meetings of my organization I was part of the 'in' crowd. Now that I'm still a member but home-bound I'm part of the 'out' crowd."

Most of us experienced that at the time of retirement some 20 years ago. Our trips back to chat with "the boys" lessened and finally ground to a halt when it dawned on us they were getting along very well without us and — could this be possible? — didn't miss us all that much. Now many 80-year olds feel that in their retirement activities they are being elbowed aside for the newly retired 60-somethings.

How do we handle this? Just as we handled it the day we discovered our former co-workers barely had time for a brief hello and a pat on the shoulder: we find new interests where our expertise is valued.

Do you have a business or a government background? Given reasonably good health, 80 is not too old to offer your services to your neighborhood school. John Glenn has been urging business and government retirees to work on programs that will pair school classes with business and government offices. The object is not to clean up parks or recycle bottles but to familiarize students with the way business and government works and to help them organize their own cooperative effort from the beginning.

You have moved away and can no longer attend the garden club where you were a member for years. You have no interest in a new one. Why not start raising some exotic houseplants? (Did you know you can grow indoor lemon trees and actually harvest ripe lemons?) Others will hear of your plants and beat a path to your door for cuttings. If you can no longer keep a dog in your apartment, team up with a friend who has a dog and visit healthcare facilities that encourage pet therapy.

My sister-in-law, Vivian, was a Navy nurse in the Phillipines during World War II. She tells of wearing Navy combat boots on duty because the crushed beach shells that covered their grounds tore their regulation nurses' shoes to shreds. When at age 90 it became difficult to be active in her retired nurses' organization, Vivian continued baking her famous orange refrigerator rolls. And when it became necessary to have help with everyday chores, Vivian first baked rolls for the two aides who came and then gave them the recipe. One of them typed off the directions from Vivian's timeworn recipe card and it has likely circled the globe by now!

Whatever we have lost in past identities is more than made up for by our new appreciation for our contemporaries, alone or in groups. We travel at the same pace, we remember most of the same things. More than ever, we are good at looking out for each other.

My friend Theresa in New York City writes wonderful letters. A former nun, Theresa knows about losses. Of her large family, seven brothers and one sister have died. Leaving the Order meant a real loss of security. Now in her 70s, she cares for a 90-year old but goes almost every day to her own little studio apartment. The street people greet her. "Hi, Mama, got some change for me? Never mind, I'll catch you on the way back."

Many letters deal with life on the New York buses. This one came just after Easter:

"I went up to the apartment on Good Friday. When I got on the bus, there were nine elderly women who seemed to be all in a group. One, who seemed to be their leader, hobbled up to ask the driver something. He asked her where they were going. She said, 'We want to go to St. Patrick's Cathedral for the Good Friday Mass.'

"The driver said, 'Yes, you could get off here but it would be a very long walk to St. Patrick's. Better you ride to the next stop and there you can catch a cross-town bus that will take you within two blocks of where you want to be.'

"At the next stop all nine shuffled to the front exit. Most of them had canes. There were people crowding to get on but the driver shouted at them, 'Get back! There are people getting off!' The group leader called out to the waiting riders, 'Somebody help us, we're all old and we need help getting off!'

"From where I was sitting all I could see were two pair of bare black arms that reached up from below. One by one they helped all the old women off. Then I heard the group leader call to the driver, 'Don't go yet!'

"'I have to go!' yelled the driver.

"'Don't go yet!' she yelled back.

"A minute later two young black men in working clothes got on, grinning broadly. One handed the driver a sheaf of bills. 'Here, they want you to have this. There's a ten spot from each of them.'

"The driver called back, 'That's not necessary!'

"The woman called back, 'Yes, it is — you were so kind. Now go buy yourself a nice dinner!'"

My adventures on Bus No. 3 pale beside Theresa's! Sometimes she gets off the bus and stops in at Jack's, a 99-cent store. In this latest letter from her I am again reminded that there are losses that never enter our minds. She writes,

"I love to go to Jack's — such bargains! I look and look. Today, cans of tuna really cheap but only one can left. I study the expiration date.

"'Hey, lady, you gonna buy that?' A six-foot, 300-pound woman is glaring down at me through gold-rimmed glasses.

"Oh, go ahead, take it. But the expiration date is 1995.'

"'Really? It's no wonder my cat won't eat that brand.' She tosses the can back on the shelf.

"I love Jacks, watching people and saving money. Today I have a sweet tooth. Kit Kats are three for a dollar and I drop three in my basket. Maybe a Nestles bar? Cocoa and marshmallows?

"'Hey, lady, you taking inventory or something? Move it!' I find myself looking down into the eyes of a midget who has his hand in my basket, pulling out Kit Kats.

"If that's what you want they're over there, three for 99 cents."

"'Easy for you to say. I can't see'em, let alone reach 'em!'

"Well, come along then. What else do you need?' We go up and down the aisles with him clutching my sleeve. Ten minutes later he's at the checkout. I wonder, can he reach? Oh, yes, he's found an empty basket and turned it over, he's standing on that and waving to me.

"'Thanks, missus! Are you married? Your children must love you!'

"I wave back but he doesn't see me. The 300-pound woman has blocked our view."

Theresa has it all — courage, daring, and an adventurous, caring heart. Having learned to put losses behind her, she has found meaning and purpose in thinking of others. She will make a splendid 80-year old!

10

*This morning there is a long e-mail from Pastor Wayne. This sur-
prises me. Isn't he scheduled for back surgery tomorrow? I print it
out; it is easier for me to read. He writes,*

"It has been three months since Larry died — no, nearly four. And
I have had a kind of break-through, an epiphany if you please, in
understanding what was going on with him in those last few weeks.
Remember how anxious he was, how desperate he was at times for
someone to be with him, to calm him?

"I couldn't understand it. He was always so upbeat. No matter how
sick he was he would say things like, 'Keep smiling!' and 'I'm ready
any time that angel wants to tap me on the shoulder.' And then,
those last weeks, he became so fragile, so distraught.

"Now I think I know what was happening. As you may know, I
have been in excruciating pain in my neck from a ruptured disk
that is resting on a nerve. When high dosages of ibuprofen didn't
come near to easing the pain, the doctor prescribed a strong synthetic
narcotic, meant to be taken over a number of days. Ten days later
the pain was bearable but the side effect of the drug was straight out
of a Stephen King novel.

"The drug made me so anxious I could not sleep or eat. I became
exhausted but as soon as I lay down on my bed I had to be up in
seconds because I could feel the room closing in on me. In the middle
of the night I would have to go outside for I felt as if everything, the
whole house, was closing in on me. It was terrifying.

"The only comfort I could find was to have Jackie with me. To be
able to lie down at all I had to have her hold me. When I was alone
I became terrified again. The drug made me crazy. I called the
doctor and said I would take the excruciating pain in preference to

this, and I went off it.

"Later it came to me: this was Larry. Those last weeks it was not the Larry we knew, it was Larry on drugs. Not the heavy pain killer, to be sure, but maybe a combination of medications that caused the same reaction. Why didn't we see it? The medical community means well but they don't know what the person is really like. They are patient, but many things they chalk up to aging. Or confusion.

"I don't know how many times Larry told me you were his anchor, his angel. He could not get through the days without you and the nights scared him silly. I know now exactly what he was saying. And this I know, if any of my parishioners are in a situation like this again, I will be there to advocate for them with a passion. How I wish I had experienced this earlier!"

The words tumble through my brain. Why didn't we see? Why weren't we more demanding? Why didn't I insist on taking him home? I could have comforted him in his night terrors. Why?

But it is over, I tell myself again and again. Larry is at peace. He is off on a magnificent adventure with Edythe and Jumping Julia and Kay Rose and all the hosts of heaven. And I will go on. I will mourn these revelations almost as much as I will grieve at his absence, but I will go on. I will forgive myself for the things I didn't know. I will work on the book again. I will tell the readers about my father-in-law and the angel. I will tidy up my desk, turn the computer on, stack these books. Ah, here is the worn little Clark book, long out of print. Glenn Clark, Methodist layman, short, stout, bald, coach of winning track teams, my mentor in college 65 years ago. I know it will fall open to the same page, the paragraph outlined by my 1935 purple-inked fountain pen:

"When you know that God is completely adequate for your needs, it is God's mind knowing through you. When you love a person to the height of oneness, it is not your little heart doing the loving, it is

really the great cosmic heart of the Infinite God flowing through you.... And certainly the Omnipotent Power that creates the miracles is not of your creation, it comes entirely from the Holy Spirit working through you." I put the book back on the pile with the others. Life is good, and every day is new.

CHAPTER TEN

In the Meantime

WHEN BILL MOYER WAS PLANNING HIS SPECIAL TV series on *Death and Dying* for PBS in 2000, he went to professionals in the field of aging to get their reactions.

"Don't do it on death and dying," they urged him. "Do it on aging." But Moyer persisted and it became one of the most-watched specials in PBS history.

Eighty-somethings are not uncomfortable with the thought of death. True, hardly a one of us looks forward to it — being alive is too marvelous! — but we have long finished pretending it doesn't exist.

When my friend Stephen was barely out of college, he rented a small apartment in a neighborhood of large, aging homes. One in particular stood out, a solid, boxy old mansion surrounded by towering elms and oaks and a high wrought iron fence. The drapes were always drawn, only a faint light escaped from around them at night. In winter snow the walks were cleared but there was never a path to the front door. Neighbors said the old man in the house had been prominent in the business and arts community but only a few of them had had so much as a glimpse of him.

Stephen often wondered about him. What an interesting man he must be, what stories he could tell! He wondered if the man were lonely. One winter Sunday, with nothing better to do, he decided to bake a blueberry pie for the old man. It was something he did well. He had his mother's prized crust recipe, he measured the fresh berries and sugar carefully, sealed the top crust down and pinched the edges together with a flair. In an hour bright magenta juice was bubbling from the fork holes in the top crust. The iron gate was unlocked and Stephen rang the bell just as the street lights came on.

The woman who answered the door wore a nurse's uniform and was clealy dubious. She looked from Stephen to the pie and back at Stephen. Then, as if some cog had slipped into place in her mind, she said abruptly, "Wait here, please," and disappeared.

When she returned, her face wore a look of bewilderment. "Follow me," she said, and then, shaking her head, "he never wants to see anyone, I can't understand. Here, this way." She took the pie.

Stephen found himself in a dimly lighted but comfortable study where an old man, slight, almost shrunken, sat in a wheelchair. A gas log glowed red in the fireplace.

"This is Stephen, a neighbor," said the nurse with forced cheerfulness. "He has brought you a blueberry pie."

The old man managed a smile. "Thank you," he said softly. He did not speak again. In a few moments the nurse brought Stephen to the door. "Come to the back door in a few days and the cook will give you your plate." Then, impulsively, "You are the first person outside the family that he has allowed inside the house for weeks!"

When Stephen came for his plate, the cook was smiling. "He didn't share that pie with no one. He said it was the best blueberry pie he'd had since he was a lad."

The long article and obituary appeared in the newspapers a few weeks later and Stephen realized who had eaten his pie. He had been in the presence of the head of one of the greatest publishing empires of the country.

For us in our eighties, death is like that man. We have never met him personally but we know people who have. We may fantasize about him and make up stories about him in our imagination, given the little real information we have. But in the back of our minds we are convinced that when we do meet he will be extraordinary and exciting, and will open worlds to us that we could never dream of!

But in the meantime — and this is the real heart of the matter — in the meantime, we will go on baking our blueberry pies and fishing for bass and raking the yard of the 90-year old across the street. The crux of the matter for us is not the meeting but the meantime.

So what do we do in the meantime?

My friend Larry, the soul of organization, had a list of businesses to be informed of his death — pensions, insurance and the like. But he also had a list of friends his sons might not know, with a column for address, another column for phone number and a final column titled, in capitals, "DATE NOTIFIED."

"Larry!" I exclaimed. "That's control beyond the grave!" But I am ready to do the same.

So make that list now. But in the meantime go to some good movies, buy a new reading lamp, send your grandkids a note of appreciation for the good people they are, give your stamp collection to the person who will most appreciate it.

Be sure all the legal issues are in place. Meanwhile, check with you doctor and then call your travel agent. Book a trip to that one place you wanted to see and never did. Buy prescription sunglasses and a gaudy umbrella.

Get rid of things you don't use. Use discretion. Eye problems prompted me to give away books early on; it will save work for someone. But Anna Hought kept her pink and white embroidered bedspread until she was 107 for it held so many memories.

Decide who should get what. Put little labels on the back if you're comfortable with that. But in the meantime, use your good dishes. Bring out your favorite drill if only to oil it. Get a massage. Phone that old schoolmate you haven't talked to in sixty years.

Give serious thought to your favorite charities, really serious. What is the very best you can do for them? In the meantime, add a hands-on project. Tutor a child or a non-English speaker. Invite some newly-arrived immigrants for tea — they rarely see the inside of an American home. Join a lecture series, sing in a choir for seniors, watch Abbot and Costello videos, join a group that puts on plays for kindergarteners, make your own note cards with art salvaged from greeting cards. Polish up your old magic tricks and entertain small children. (The travelers to Bethlehem were magicians — magi — who had seen a great light.) Write a novel. Get involved in politics. Laugh more, sleep less, move about more, stretch often.

If your fingers are arthritic, ask a grandchild or a friend to type off your Christmas card list on labels to save you all the addressing. Save your fingers to write personal notes on each card or at the end of your dittoed letter. I try to pare down my list but I can't — I want to know what's happening in every one of their lives.

Finally, if you are disturbed about the big question, if your spiritual roadmap isn't clear enough to tell you what you're really expecting to find at the end of the route, talk to someone. Talk to your pastor, or your rabbi, or to a trusted friend. Hospice can often refer you to someone helpful.

My own comfortable approach to life after death is based not on theology or even on my own personal faith in the love of God, but on something my father-in-law told me over coffee on a summer afternoon in 1941.

Edwin was a Minnesota farmer, a plain dirt farmer, as the saying goes. A son of immigrants, one of a large family, I think he disliked farming but he was trapped. During the terrible years of the depression and drought of the 1930's he lost the family farm. In 1940 he was trying desperately to buy it back from the Federal Land Bank. He was already steeped in worry when, in January of 1941, his beloved Anna suffered a severe stroke that left her bed-ridden. Marian, one of the daughters who was a nurse, came home to care for her.

But there was more. In a family whose life revolved around the country church a half mile away, Edwin had had a falling out with that church. For more than a year he had refused to step inside the door or speak to the pastor. I never knew the reason. If anyone did, they never spoke of it. Perhaps it was the new fire and brimstone pastor, who let it be known that anyone who didn't come to prayer meeting or offer a "testimony" when called upon did not belong in the fold. Edwin was a man of few words.

His gloom grew deeper. Today I think we would say he was severely depressed. And when Anna died in the summer of 1941, just as her stand of rugosa roses were bursting into bloom, we held our breaths, wondering what would happen to Edwin now.

But Edwin was a changed man. He smiled. He was cheerful. He seemed downright happy. We were almost embarrassed — is this a way to grieve? He went back to church, even on the Sunday before the funeral! He was expansive, almost effusive, in welcoming his brothers who came from Canada for the service.

Two or three weeks later he drove in to town from the farm and tapped on my door. "Is the coffee pot on?" We sat at the kitchen table. I brought out cream for his coffee. "Old farm boys, you can't change them!" We talked about the weather, the haying.

Suddenly he leaned across the table. "I have to tell you something, I have seen an angel!" His eyes shone. His thick black hair, which never grayed until he was almost 90, framed his tanned face like a halo.

This is how he told it. The morning of Anna's death he had risen early, as he always did. He made a fire in the kitchen range, cooked a pot of coffee and drank a cup. Then, as he always did, he brought a cup to Anna and sat with her while she drank it in bed. Before waking the rest of the household — Marian, son Lenus and the hired hand — he always went out to the wooded pasture himself and brought the cows back to the barn for milking.

"That morning when I came into the barnyard, I glanced up at the house. And as plain as I see you sitting there, just as plain as that, I saw an angel on the peak of the roof! And I knew that Anna was gone."

He ran to the house. Yes, Anna had died while he was getting the cows.

Why didn't we talk about it more? Why didn't we tell everyone? Why didn't he? Why didn't I? Talking to family members in later years, I think I'm the only one he told it to. It may have been that, recently married, I was new to the family; sometimes we are afraid that people who have known us well will dismiss us too quickly.

And it might have been easy to dismiss it as a reaction to worry and grief over Anna's death, to say his mind formed a mirage to protect itself from so much pain. No, that would never have accounted for the change in the man. He was new. He was different. Anyone seeing him that day with his coffee growing cold in front of him would have known. And the change lasted a lifetime. He had seen an angel!

For a long time it was a great comfort to me. If an angel came to escort Anna to heaven, then angels will come for us, too. It has taken until my eighties to understand that the angel didn't come for Anna, he came for Edwin.

Anna didn't need an angel. With her tremendous faith and dedication, Anna would find her own way to heaven in the same way she found her way to the door to the church basement, carrying a covered dish. (Garrison Keillor insists that Lutheran women, when they reach heaven, will head for the basement door for they will be carrying a hot dish. The women of Anna's church used to say, "If you're asking Anna for a cake you'll need one less because she always make a double recipe.")

But Edwin desperately needed an angel that year. I like to think it was an answer to Anna's last wish, her last prayer that morning after Edwin carried her coffee cup back to the kitchen.

"Immortality" is not a word Edwin would have used. It was enough for him that he had seen an angel.

And even for us 80-somethings who have already lived so long, the idea is hard to internalize. Life has always held beginnings and ends — seed time and harvest, births and deaths. We anticipate immortality through belief or by faith, but we also find comfort in its more immediate expressions.

Perhaps Vivian's refrigerator rolls are the sort of immortality we handle best. Her recipe dates back at least one generation, likely two, for it reads, "Put in icebox overnight." If in her 90s she gives it to her children, her grandchildren and their children, these directions for a simple breakfast treat will have passed through six generations and almost 200 years.

So, too, we transmit the strengths we have gained from our family past and from our own 80-some years. By action or words we pass on our faith, optimism, durability, love of truth, patience and courage. It is our personal, present and joyous hold on the flame of immortality.

It's enough. In our eighties, with so many loose ends neatly tied, with such imaginative and creative things yet to do, with tremendous expectations, we are truly in the "best decade" now!

NOTE 1:

As this book goes to the printer, the Harvard Study on Adult Development has just been published, the longest-running study ever made on aging. *Aging Well* by study director George Valiant, M.D., is a fascinating examination of "why some of us get better with age." I would urge you to call your library or local bookstore and reserve a copy.

From that book, two points to ponder:

- It is not the bad things that happen to us that doom us, it is the good people that happen to us that facilitate enjoyable old age.

- Healing relationships are facilitated by a capacity for gratitude, for forgiveness, and for taking people inside (becoming emotionally enriched by them).

VIVIAN'S COFFEE BREAD

3/4 cup Crisco

3/4 cup sugar

1 cup boiling water

2 well-beaten eggs

2 pkgs. yeast dissolved in 1 cup lukewarm water

6 cups flour

2 teaspoons salt

Cream together Crisco and sugar. Pour boiling water over this and mix. When cool add well-beaten eggs and yeast dissolved in 1 cup lukewarm water. Sift 2 cups of the flour with salt, add and stir, then BEAT in 2 cups and stir in last 2.) Cover bowl with a wet towel and refrigerate overnight or at least 2 hours. (Vivian's original recipe said "Put in icebox.")

This can be made into coffee bread, dinner rolls, cinnamon rolls. Vivian said she makes one loaf pan of coffee bread and the rest in orange rolls. For these, mix 5 tablespoons butter with 1/2 cup sugar and grated rind of one orange (save some of rind to mix with powdered sugar frosting after baking). Roll dough into a rectangle, spread with orange mix. Roll like a jelly roll and slice. Arrange in pan and bake 20 to 25 minutes at 350°. The dough does not have to rise before going into the oven. If you don't have an orange, a lemon will do — you'll have lemon rolls!

Index

1. Appreciating: *The Best Decade* 11

2. Grounding: *Dr. Livingston, I Assume?* 19

3. Changing: *The Day Connie Shot the Squirrel* 27

4. Moving: *Change of Address* 37

5. Coping: *Gabriella, Who Danced on the Ceiling* 47

6. Walking: *Bless My Sole* 59

7. Balancing: *Mixed Messages* 71

8. Remembering:
   The Priest Who Walked Through the Window 83

9. Finding: *Lost and Found* 97

10. Anticipating: *In the Meantime* 109

Order Form

BookMasters, Inc.

P.O. Box 2139

Mansfield, OH 44905

Please send _____ copies of "How to Get From 80 to 90 Without Even Trying", price $12.95, to the address below. I include $2.95 for handling and mailing up to (and including) three books.

Name _____

Address _____

City _____ State _____ Zip _____

To order by phone: 1-800-537-6727

To order by e-mail: info@bookmasters.com